HUNGRY

HUNGRY

LEARNING TO FEED YOUR
SOUL WITH **CHRIST**

RONDI LAUTERBACH

P&R
PUBLISHING
P.O. BOX 817 • PHILLIPSBURG • NEW JERSEY 08865-0817

Printed in the United States of America

Library of Congress Cataloging-in-Publication Data

Names: Lauterbach, Rondi, author.
Title: Hungry : learning to feed your soul with Christ / Rondi Lauterbach.
Description: Phillipsburg : P&R Publishing, 2016.
Identifiers: LCCN 2016017563| ISBN 9781629952017 (pbk.) | ISBN 9781629952024 (epub) | ISBN 9781629952031 (mobi)
Subjects: LCSH: Spiritual life--Christianity.
Classification: LCC BV4501.3 .L3845 2016 | DDC 248.4--dc23
LC record available at https://lccn.loc.gov/2016017563

To my husband, Mark,
who has nourished and cherished me these thirty-eight years

Contents

Tables

Foreword

What's more satisfying than sitting down to a sumptuous feast that's been prepared by a skilled master chef? Everything about that kind of eating is inviting: the aromas, the pairings, the platings, even the table settings. Some of that food is so beautiful that I hate to destroy the artistry by eating it, but it smells so good that I can't resist!

There are people (both women and men) who love to create lovely meals, who use that exercise as an expression of their love and creativity. I am thankful for them, but that's just not my gifting.

This is more how it goes around my house: shocked that it's already a quarter to five, I grab the frozen hamburger out of the freezer, nuke it in the microwave for five minutes, and slap it on the skillet with leftover chopped onion and Hamburger Helper. Then I snatch the bag of salad out of the veggie drawer—sometimes checking the use-by date—rip it open, douse it with the dregs of questionable ranch dressing, pile it all on a plate, and call, "Dinner's ready!" as we take up our positions in front of the five o'clock television news program.

Is that kind of eating actually nourishing? Sure it is . . . sort of. But it certainly isn't anything you'll remember the day after. In fact, you might try to forget it. (And we haven't even mentioned the many days when my "cooking" takes the form of whatever my new favorite fast food restaurant happens to be.)

I just asked what was better than a sumptuous feast, lovingly prepared. Here's the answer: a feast on the Word of God.

Christians know that they should read the Bible regularly. That's kind of a no-brainer, isn't it? Since God has condescended to lay before us an assortment of such delicious words, we ought to slow down to really enjoy them. But we already know that, don't we? So we cram in reading as best we can, sometimes just so that we won't feel bad about not reading *again*.

Sometimes we read our Bibles the way I prepare dinner. You know the drill: It's six forty-five in the morning, and we know that the gang will be up at seven o'clock, the day will blast off, and the next time we'll have an opportunity even to breathe won't be until we fall exhaustedly into bed fifteen hours later when the thought of reading anything with understanding is laughable. But . . . *I've only got fifteen minutes,* we might think. *How can I do anything of any import in that short time?*

It's easy to assume that if we had an hour to study the Bible, we could really get something out of it. But since a full hour of uninterrupted thought is as scarce in our homes as a beautifully plated filet mignon, we cram as much as we can into the twelve minutes that we now have left and hope that something sticks.

But, honestly, we can't figure out how reading a two-thousand-year-old letter from Paul to a slave owner is supposed to make any sense to us at all . . . and by the time we get done with even a tiny New Testament book like Philemon, we're more confused than ever. *If only I had more time to study, I'd do better with this; I bet I would understand it*, we think. But more time never comes.

And then there are those bleak fast-food days when we don't even pick up our Bibles at all but rather tune in to a podcast and hope that some sustenance gets into our starving souls through iTunes. We consistently find ourselves *hungry* for something more but don't know how to stop that craving in the time that we've got.

You may not need to read another book about how the Bible is the Word of God. I may not need to tell you that you ought to read it. Perhaps you already know that and already feel pretty bad about how you're doing it. The problem is not always with knowing that we should read and digest God's Word; the problem is with how to do it in the time that we have *and* to stay motivated.

That's where this immensely helpful book comes in. My friend Rondi Lauterbach has lovingly, beautifully, and wisely plated all the ingredients you'll need in order to begin studying your Bible, even if (*especially if*) all you have is fifteen minutes every day. Using the paradigm of cooking a nutritious meal, along with the book of Philemon, Rondi is going to help you to learn how to read *and* really digest the Word of Life.

But that's not all that she's going to do. She'll also accomplish something that most writers of Bible study books fail to do: she'll help you to see Jesus, the true Bread, the Living Word, on every page . . . and in that, she'll give you a unique motivation to keep on. You don't read your Bible just so you can cross it off your daily list or learn some new steps so that your life will finally become what you hoped it would be. You read, study, digest it so that you can feast on Jesus, the one who loves you, who will speak to you, and who gave his body and blood for your life.

Shockingly, Jesus is the missing ingredient in nearly all books about Bible study; aside from a gospel sprinkling here or a "remember the cross" thought there, you'd think that he wasn't the main point of Scripture. But he is. And Rondi won't let you push him aside or pick around him. He's there on every page in Scripture, as he said he was, and Rondi will continue to present him to you so that you will be motivated by his love, his life, and his delight in you and will learn to satisfy your hunger with the only meal that can actually do so.

So pull up a chair. Get ready to feast. Hope you've come hungry. You're about to be fed a supremely delicious meal.

Enjoy!

Elyse M. Fitzpatrick
Author of *Idols of the Heart*

Introduction

Running on Empty

For he satisfies the longing soul,
and the hungry soul he fills with good things.
—Psalm 107:9

Imagine I see my son late one night when I walk into the kitchen to get some water. The refrigerator bulb illuminates his face as he stares blankly ahead. Cold air pours past him. "Mom. There's no food in this house."

I wrap my robe more tightly and peer into our moderately stocked refrigerator. *Poor starving teenager. His hunger drives him to forage for food every three hours. It's like having a newborn again.*

"Actually, there's a sandwich in here waiting for you to find it. Look. There's the bread; here's some leftover turkey. You could add cream cheese, some of that cranberry sauce, and a bit of lettuce, and you've got a Thanksgiving sandwich. It's all in there; you just have to learn to see the makings of a meal."

He stares at me, then starts grabbing ingredients with both hands. In minutes he is wolfing down a monstrous sandwich, sighing with pleasure.

Score one for Mom.

HUNGRY BODIES

A mom expects her kids to get hungry. After all, a healthy appetite is a sign of life. She plans for their hunger so she won't get caught by surprise. She keeps Cheerios in the diaper bag, pretzel packets in her purse, energy bars in her car. A mom is prepared because she knows that hunger can hit anyone without warning. Even her.

I'm one of those people who get low blood sugar. It can plummet suddenly when I'm in the middle of an exercise class or out running errands. It's as though a gas tank needle suddenly drops below empty. I'm often surprised by the urgent need to stop and refuel.

One day my need hit me on the way home from work. I had planned to run by the cleaners, mail a package, and pick up a few items for dinner. By the third stop, brain fog hit. *I'm not going to make it.*

Fortunately, I was at the grocery store. *Good. I'll pick up some protein bars and eat one right away.* I headed to the far right aisle. *I forgot—they've rearranged the store. I think they're on the other side. I'll get them on the way out.* I picked up the three items on my list and circled to the other side of the store. No protein bars. I was getting desperate, so I grabbed the first thing I saw that qualified as instant food: maple leaf cookies.

Cookies for dinner. That's what happens when hunger catches me off guard.

Hunger is definitely a driving force in our lives. Have you ever whipped into the drive-thru at McDonald's because your detox diet left you craving french fries? Or stood over the sink eating ice cream out of the carton at midnight because dinner didn't quite do it for you?

If hunger can drive our bodies like that, what does it do to our souls?

HUNGRY SOULS

During my teen years, I not only had a taste for potato chips and M&M's but also developed an appetite for achievement. I had begged my parents to let me switch from my sheltered church school to a large public high school. After checking it out thoroughly, they consented, but with a few stipulations. "You have to take your schoolwork seriously. We expect you to keep up your grades and stay on track for college."

I did what I was told and pleased my parents by performing well. But the truth was, the more I filled myself up with achievement, the more I craved it. Before long I was addicted to success and the kudos that accompanied it. On the outside I was a good and cheerful student, a credit to my school and my parents, but on the inside things weren't so pretty.

Addicts know well the law of diminishing returns. It seemed that every day I had to prove myself all over again. I had to stay ahead of the competition. I soon began getting up at four in the morning to study, popping prescription meds to stay awake and increase my concentration. Anxiety churned and sometimes surfaced as panic. The next award satisfied me only briefly before the growling emptiness drove me into another whirl of effort.

I was running on empty.

What about you? Do you know when your soul is hungry? I wasn't aware of my drivenness, though it was probably obvious to the people around me. You may find yourself suddenly getting irritated by every little thing. You may become easily offended, reacting in anger to your family, picking fights with your friends, neighbors, even strangers. *What's wrong with me?*

Our souls are a swamp of feelings. Vague dissatisfactions cloud the surface while deep longings—for truth, affirmation, friends, significance, peace—rise briefly and then sink again.

They pull us under. We surface, gasping and lurching for the first thing we see.

We act out of hunger before we realize what we're feeling.

HOPE FOR THE HUNGRY

The connection between physical and spiritual hunger is on our society's radar these days. Popular author and physician Deepak Chopra hands us the appropriate diagnostic question "What am I hungry for?" and goes on to answer it this way:

> The impulse you feel can be simplified into a few basic categories:
> *You're hungry for food.*
> *You want to fill an emotional hole.*
> *You want to fill a hole in your mind* (such as low self-esteem, bad body image, or a sense of failure or frustration).
> To these I would add a fourth impulse, which is spiritual.
> *You want to fill a hole in your soul.*[1]

His diagnosis is accurate. Not just our bodies, emotions, and minds but also our very souls are hungry. We want to fill a hole in our souls.

But Chopra's prescription isn't deep enough. In an earlier book he counsels us to look within. He recommends self-awareness through spiritual practices such as yoga, meditation, and mindfulness. According to Chopra, our self-awareness has been contracted by problems of various kinds. We need to move from "contracted awareness" to "expanded awareness" with the goal of "pure awareness."[2] This is his spiritual solution to our hunger problem.

---

1. Deepak Chopra, *What Are You Hungry For? The Chopra Solution to Permanent Weight Loss, Well-Being, and Lightness of Soul* (New York: Harmony Books, 2013), 16 (italics in original).
2. Deepak Chopra, *Spiritual Solutions: Answers to Life's Greatest Challenges* (New York: Harmony Books, 2012), 4–7.

Self-awareness might help us to diagnose our hunger, but looking inside ourselves for the answer assumes that we can fill our own souls. But how can we do this? When our stomachs are empty, we don't turn inward. We open the refrigerator.

Where do we go to find food for our souls?

The Bible takes this question seriously. One day a large crowd goes looking for Jesus (John 6:25–40). The people's stomachs are empty, and they're hoping that he'll feed them again as he did the day before, when he turned five loaves and two fish into enough to satisfy them all. Today they want more bread. Another miracle might be nice too—entertainment with the meal.

Jesus knows what they want. He sees the crowd. He hears the question behind their question, "Lord, when did you get here?" He is well aware of their hunger.

Jesus also knows that bread isn't what the people need. Their stomachs will feel empty again in a few hours. Entertainment won't satisfy them either. Their curiosity will soon demand another sign of his power. They need food for a hunger that they're not yet aware of.

So Jesus says to them, "I am the bread of life; whoever comes to me shall not hunger, and whoever believes in me shall never thirst" (v. 35).

In saying this, Jesus is telling the crowd two things.

First, Jesus is telling the people that he is aware of their true need, even if they aren't. He knows that they need food for their souls, that they have a hunger to be fully alive. They don't need to become self-aware, because he is aware for them and is compassionate enough to tell them what he knows.

Second, Jesus is saying that he is ready and able to provide for their true hunger. He knows that bread will keep them alive only one day at a time—merely surviving. But the bread he offers will allow them to live with a capital *L*—thriving. Jesus doesn't stop at giving the crowd self-awareness and then send them off on a spiritual quest. He offers to provide for their hungry souls.

And the bread that he offers is himself.

The people are baffled by his words, and I think that his words sometimes go over our heads too. But Jesus lets his announcement hang in the air, for their sake and for ours.

FEED ME

Jesus is the Bread of Life. Those words were shockingly good news to me as a teenager. I'd been feeding on achievement, and all it had brought me was more hunger. This wasn't life; it was addiction, "a banquet in the grave."[3]

Jesus offered me the gift of life in exchange for the law of diminishing returns that I had embraced. He called me not just to hear his words but to feed on them—to take them seriously, to believe they were true, to be convinced of them personally. He called me not just to feed on his words but also to feed on *him*. That meant to take him seriously, to understand who he claimed to be and what he came to do, and to place my trust in him.

I barely understood the message, but God helped me to believe and, by believing, to feed on Jesus as my Bread of Life for the first time. As it turned out, I would need to feed on him again.

In my thirties I went through a personal crisis. Motherhood had disturbed more than my comfort; it had challenged my sense of identity. I had done well in school and had always assumed I would have a successful career someday. Kids? Of course I would have a few of those too. That's what the culture told me at the time: you can have it all—kids, career, happiness,

---

3. I borrowed this phrase from Edward T. Welch's book on addiction, *Addictions—A Banquet in the Grave: Finding Hope in the Power of the Gospel* (Phillipsburg, NJ: P&R Publishing, 2001).

fulfillment. I swallowed that line, finished college, and settled into graduate school. The first baby arrived. Then two more.

I was up to my ears in diapers, toddlers, sticky fingers, and runny noses. How was I supposed to concentrate on anything else, much less on a career? Maybe when the children started school I would have the mental bandwidth. So I kept putting it off, thinking that my time would come. I embraced being a mom, but motherhood didn't feel like enough. I wanted to make something of myself.

The crisis hit. The last child entered grade school. I found myself with a chunk of free time each day to use as I wished, but in agony I realized that I didn't know what to do with it. Where was that career that would fill the empty spot? My children still needed me to be available to them. What fabulous job would fit my limited schedule and also fill the hole in my soul?

I didn't want a career; I craved an identity.

Who am I? The question haunted me. Sometimes in the middle of the night I would dream I was falling into a dark well and would wake up with a start, terrified. My soul felt like a black hole, sucking me downward.

I read my Bible. Tried to pray. Journaled my despair. Then, one gray and dreary morning, the Holy Spirit quietly brought Christ's words to my mind: *I am the Bread of Life.* It felt so personal—the very words I needed to hear.

I knew those words. I believed they were true. But that day the Spirit of God spoke them to me again. I took them from the page of my Bible and began to feed on them. I had been looking for life in so many places for so long, and all the while Jesus had been holding out his life to me with both hands.

That day I learned that Jesus' life isn't just my rescue from achievement addiction—it is my very identity. And it is mine for the taking, not just today but tomorrow and all the days after.

That's Jesus' offer to all who are hungry: a present-tense, life-sustaining relationship with him.

BRING YOUR HUNGRY

I assume that you picked up this book because you're hungry. You might consider yourself an outsider to the Christian faith, or you might be a committed insider. You might even be straddling the boundary line of faith, shifting your weight from one foot to the other. But one thing is certain: you're hungry.

Welcome to the table.

Together we're going to explore what the Bible has to say about hunger, both physical and spiritual. Together we're going to ask questions, such as:

- Does my hunger matter to God?
- Is hunger good or bad?
- How can I recognize my hunger? Understand it? Satisfy it?
- Where can I find food?

The Bible has a lot to say about hunger and even more to say about food. It has the most to say about a God who wants to feed us. We've come to the right place for our search, "for he satisfies the longing soul, and the hungry soul he fills with good things" (Ps. 107:9).

Here's the menu.

- *Part 1: Hunger.* We'll learn where our hunger comes from and why it feels insatiable. We'll consider the story of the God who gives birth to his children and then feeds them. We'll talk about the surprising role of the wilderness, the problem of cravings, and our hope of satisfaction. I've also included some questions at the end of each chapter for personal reflection or discussion in a group setting.

- *Part 2: Plenty.* We'll learn how to find food for ourselves from the Bible. We'll learn to cook this meal together. I'll give you tools, and we'll practice our skills. But we won't stop until this feast tastes right—sweet as honey—which means that we'll need to learn to see Jesus, hear the good news, and taste his grace on every page of the Book.

That's what I plan to bring to the table. What about you? What are you bringing to the table? Ponder that for a minute and scribble a thought or two at the bottom of this page.

Then come. Bring your hungry to his plenty.

PART ONE

HUNGER

One

Hunger

The belly is an ungrateful wretch, it never remembers
past favors, it always wants more tomorrow.
—*Aleksandr Solzhenitsyn,* One Day in
the Life of Ivan Denisovich

When I think of being driven by hunger, I picture Lucky, our fat old beagle.

We bought him because beagles make the cutest puppies. What we didn't realize is that beagles are essentially noses attached to stomachs—rather large stomachs, I might add.

Lucky had no brain, only an appetite. That meant he had one mission in life—whenever the front door opened, he bolted out of it, nose first, in search of food. There was no way to catch him. We tried, of course, cruising around the neighborhood in our car, windows down, listening for the baying voice that gave away his position. But he always eluded us.

One evening after we had given Lucky up for coyote bait, we looked out our kitchen window to see him trot up the driveway with a package of fresh hot dog buns dangling from his mouth. Since the grocery store was four miles away, we figured that he had swiped them out of the back of some woman's minivan while she was taking groceries inside. We pictured her scratching her head, wondering if she was going crazy, when she couldn't find those buns at dinnertime.

Another time, I didn't realize that Lucky was gone until I got a phone call from the nearby junior high school. "Hey, lady, are you the one who owns the beagle? You need to come and get him; he just ate a piece of cake off a teacher's desk . . ."

"What am I hungry for?" would have been a meaningless question for our beagle. He never stopped long enough to ask it.

DEEP HUNGER

But we do. When we find ourselves rummaging in the refrigerator but can't seem to settle on what we want, we ask it. When we find ourselves restless, moving from room to room without settling down, we ask it. When we find ourselves obsessing over yesterday's job interview or the sharp comment that our best friend made to us last week, we ask it.

What am I hungry for? Our uncomfortable feelings are symptoms of a strong desire or need for something that we haven't yet named. A battery of blood tests can diagnose a nutritional deficiency, but it's not always easy for us to name our other hungers. We're always on the prowl for a label that fits us.

Name That Hunger

A smartly dressed young woman was chatting with me before a weekend retreat in British Columbia. She had just landed a high-profile job in a marketing firm downtown. Giggling nervously, she admitted, "I feel like an impostor. They all think I know what I'm doing, but I don't. I'm afraid they'll find out!"

I could relate to her lack of self-confidence, but I had never thought of myself as an *impostor* before. What an intriguing label. When I looked it up later, I found that *impostor* was more than a well-chosen word—it had been identified as a syndrome.

The term *impostor syndrome* was coined in the 1970s to describe the experience of people who are convinced that they are incompetent despite evidence to the contrary. Instead of accepting the evidence, they dismiss it, assuming that they've tricked everyone into thinking that they're smarter or better qualified than they actually are.[1]

That seals it, I thought to myself like a psychological hypochondriac. *I think I've got a case of impostor syndrome! Now what can I do about it?*

Wonder Woman

Taking my self-diagnosed hunger for self-confidence in hand, I began to research my condition. I read about a variety of management techniques, but the one that I liked best came from the research of Harvard assistant professor Amy Cuddy.

In 2012 Dr. Cuddy gave a talk about power poses and the difference they can make in our sense of self-assurance. With research to back up her claims, she showed that how we stand, sit, and walk affects hormonal levels in our blood that in turn affect our mood. Standing like Wonder Woman for two minutes— hands on hips, feet wide—actually boosts our confidence by measurable levels. Her TED talk must have hit a nerve, because it went viral and now has over thirty million views.[2]

Impostor syndrome therapies and Dr. Cuddy's research have been helpful to many people. Managing our confidence is useful when we have a specific task in front of us that must be

1. Carl Richards, "Learning to Deal With the Impostor Syndrome," *The New York Times*, October 26, 2015, http://www.nytimes.com/2015/10/26/your-money/learning-to-deal-with -the-impostor-syndrome.html?_r=0.
2. Amy Cuddy, "Your Body Language Shapes Who You Are" (TEDGlobal, 2012), video, *TED*, 21:02, last accessed April 25, 2016, http://www.ted.com/talks/amy_cuddy_your_body _language_shapes_who_you_are?language=en.

done. But we eventually find that our hunger for confidence goes deeper than the specific circumstances that provoked it. It seems to linger long after the job is done. It pops up again at unexpected times.

Managing this hunger doesn't satisfy it.

Why Am I Hungry?

We need to ask a deeper question than "What am I hungry for?" because we need to find a deeper answer. That question is *why*. Why are you and I hungry for self-confidence—or for anything else? And why won't that hunger stay satisfied?

Five hundred years ago, a young Bible scholar began what was to be his life's work with these words: "Nearly all the wisdom we possess, that is to say, true and sound wisdom, consists of two parts: the knowledge of God and of ourselves."[3]

He went on to say that we can't know God without knowing ourselves and that we can't know ourselves without knowing God. The two are connected. They're actually interrelated. You can't have one without the other.

Where should we start, then? That was John Calvin's question too: "But as these are connected together by many ties, it is not easy to determine which of the two precedes and gives birth to the other." Our hunger can provide an entry point. One way to know ourselves is to begin to take our hunger seriously—to recognize it, understand it, and ask why.

When we realize that our diagnosis of hunger is superficial and our strategies for treatment inadequate, we begin to look around for help. Eventually we look up. "For, in the first place, no man can survey himself without forthwith turning his thoughts toward God in whom he lives and moves." We find ourselves

---

3. This and the following three quotations are from John Calvin, *Institutes of the Christian Religion*, trans. Henry Beveridge (Peabody, MA: Hendrickson Publishers, 2007), 1.1.1.

seeking God, and then, to our surprise, we find him looking down to seek us.

"Every person, therefore, on coming to the knowledge of himself, is not only urged to seek God, but is also led as by the hand to find him." One way to know God and ourselves is to follow the breadcrumb trail of our hunger through the pages of the Bible.

Why am I hungry? Let's take that question with us as we open the Book.

HUNGER BEGUN

Genesis, the first book of the Bible, means *beginning*. It's a good place to start our quest to understand hunger. The first chapter of Genesis opens with these words: "In the beginning, God created the heavens and the earth" (Gen. 1:1).

Whether we are reading these words for the first or for the hundredth time, we can observe one thing right away. God is assumed. He exists before everything else. His presence is stated as a given, without apology or explanation. You could say that he stands alone on the stage, except that there is no stage yet.

The second thing we see from this single sentence is that God made everything else—the theater, the stage, the scenery, the props, the players, you, me. There's one major distinction introduced here: God and everything else. The Creator and everything he created. This may seem obvious, but it's pertinent to our discussion of hunger.

God Is Never Hungry

Here's the implication: God is not hungry. Not ever. Not for anything. Hunger describes us but not him.

The idea that God doesn't need anything recurs throughout the Bible. The clearest explanation comes centuries later in these words spoken by a converted Jew named Paul to the cosmopolitan citizens of Athens:

> The God who made the world and everything in it, being Lord of heaven and earth, does not live in temples made by man, nor is he served by human hands, as though he *needed* anything, since he himself *gives* to all mankind life and breath and everything. (Acts 17:24–25)

God is the one who gives, not the one who needs.

But there's more. God is not just "not hungry"; he is satisfied, utterly satisfied. That's the positive way to put an absence of hunger. God is satisfied in every area in which we are needy. We long for meaning, identity, purpose. We long for relationships of mutual love, honor, and respect. We need these things to make us feel fully alive. God doesn't need these things to feel fully alive, because he already has them. He is as fully alive as it gets.

You might argue with me here. "I can see that God doesn't need food," you might say, "but what about relationships? Since God is alone on the stage, he might be, well, lonely. Perhaps he created the world to fill that one need?" That's good reasoning. And that's one of the ways in which Genesis 1 points to the true nature of God as one God in three persons.[4]

The fact is that our hunger plunges us into the deep end of the pool, into the very nature of God himself. We are so needy

---

4. Genesis 1:26 is another pointer: "Then God said, 'Let us make man in our image, after our likeness.'" Why does God refer to himself with the plural pronouns *us* and *our?* Genesis 1:2 offers a partial explanation: "And the Spirit of God was hovering over the face of the waters." The Spirit of God is also there. Genesis 1:3 gives the third clue: "And God said, 'Let there be light.'" The Word of God is present too. The Triune nature of God, hinted at in the Old Testament, is made clear in the New Testament—e.g., Matthew 3:16–17 (the baptism of Jesus); Matthew 28:19 (the triune name of God); 2 Corinthians 13:14 (the triune blessing).

that we need to receive help from someone who isn't needy in the least. God is that someone. He doesn't need a relationship with us because he existed in a perfect relationship of mutual love, honor, and respect *before* the beginning, as Father, Son, and Spirit. Alone (one God) but not lonely (three persons).

In other words, the triune God is not only complete, he's completely happy. "God is that being who exists as the triune love of the Father for the Son in the unity of the Spirit. The boundless life that God lives in himself, at home, within the happy land of the Trinity above all worlds, is perfect. It is complete, inexhaustibly full, and infinitely blessed."[5]

This is the God who is presented to us in the first sentence of the book of beginnings.

Food for the Hungry

Turning back to Genesis,[6] let's keep our eyes peeled for anything related to hunger.

The story of God's creation of all things unfolds over the next two chapters, first in poetry, then in prose. In chapter 1 we see him building the structures of our world and filling them with life. The poet seems to craft his account to show that the one who creates life also sustains it. Like a good host, God provides food before the guests arrive.

Thus we read that all plant life is created on day three, in preparation for the arrival of animal life, including us, on day six. Then God connects the dots between our hunger and his provision. "Behold," he says, and it's as though he makes a sweeping gesture to the vast array of plant life, then turns to the man and the woman. "You shall have them for food" (Gen. 1:29).

---

5. Fred Sanders, *The Deep Things of God: How the Trinity Changes Everything* (Wheaton, IL: Crossway, 2010), 62.

6. If you don't have a Bible available, you can look up the book of Genesis on Bible Gateway (www.biblegateway.com). I'm using the English Standard Version (ESV) in this book.

All the animals, as well as man and woman, would be fed from this abundance.

The need was met before the need was felt. In creation, God made food first, then made creatures with an appetite. In paradise, hunger is always satisfied.

God Made Me to Hunger

What does that mean for us? It tells us where hunger comes from. We are beings who need to eat. If we don't have food, we get hungry, weak, and faint, and eventually we die.

God made us that way. He could have created beings that don't need nourishment, like a rock or a perpetual motion machine. He could have made us self-sustaining, able to produce our own food within ourselves. He could have made us to need food only once a month or once a year.

But he didn't. He chose to make us creatures who wake up hungry every day and have to grab breakfast before we head out the door.

This tells us several more things about us, our hunger, and the God who feeds us.

We're dependent on something outside ourselves to sustain our lives. Remember, we go to the pantry, not to our inner selves, when our stomachs rumble. This fact, so obvious in the physical realm, gets muddled when we think about spirituality. But we are not self-sustaining spiritually any more than we are physically. Our souls' food is *out there*, not in here.

Hunger is good. What would our lives be like if we didn't have an appetite? We get a small taste of this when we have the flu. Nothing tastes right, and we don't feel like eating. But when our appetite returns, even a piece of buttered toast tastes incredible. A good appetite is the best thing to bring to the table.

God is good. He creates desires that he plans to satisfy. Our appetite is more than matched by his provision. The abundance and variety of physical food on this planet shows his generosity. He made food for us to *enjoy*,[7] not just to subsist on.

But God has other food for us that he doesn't give to the animals. He made us for a relationship with himself.

HUNGER TESTED

As we move from Genesis 1 to Genesis 2, we encounter one more word about food, which points beyond our physical hunger. God speaks to the man again:

> And the LORD God commanded the man, saying, "You may surely eat of every tree of the garden, but of the tree of the knowledge of good and evil you shall not eat, for in the day that you eat of it you shall surely die." (Gen. 2:16–17)

Before the woman is created, God speaks to the man, giving a command (really two): "You may surely eat" and "You shall not eat."

Now, if you're an outsider to Christianity, these words may seem to confirm your suspicions about religion. God sounds like a cosmic killjoy. First he gives, then he says, "Don't touch!" Why the generous provision and then the one prohibition? Why make any rules at all?

What might sound at first like a power play is actually an offer, an invitation for the man to bring his deep hungers to the table. Paradise won't be complete as long as the man is alone. But before God creates the woman to satisfy that loneliness, he

---

7. ". . . God, who richly provides us with everything to enjoy" (1 Tim. 6:17).

offers the man a relationship with himself. God's command is the offer. Adam's obedience is how he will say yes.

"But," you may ask, "what do rules have to do with a relationship?"

Everything. Rules tell us how to please the one we love.

Rules of Relationship

When we fall in love with someone, funny things can happen. I once developed a crush on a boy who loved to play basketball. At that point I was a bookworm who didn't know what to do with myself when Mom said, "Go outside and play," except to take my book outside and read there. But once I began to like this neighbor boy, I started to dribble and shoot like nobody's business. If he liked basketball, by golly, I was going to like it too.

That relationship didn't pan out, but when love blossomed between my husband Mark and me years later, the scenario replayed itself—not with basketball but with wanting to please the other person. I offered to take up golf. He offered to take me dancing.

Other rules developed over time. If he wanted to show that he loved me, he needed to buy me the right kind of hand lotion when I sent him to the store. Not the cheapest kind, not the kind that he thought was best, but the kind that I asked him to get. If I wanted to show that I loved him, I needed to keep our dog Lucky from digging up the drip irrigation line. Not just to let him out and forget about him, but to take him out, watch him, and bring him in.

All this wasn't about the hand lotion or the drip line; it was about the person. The rule says, "This is important to me." How I respond to the rule shows what I think of the person.

The Purpose of Hunger

Here is the test that God sets up for the man: "I have given you everything you need. More than you need. But you must know that life comes from me, not just from these things. The way to choose life is to choose me, to love me more than you love the things I give you."

Now, remember who we're talking about. God isn't some lonely teenager with pimples. He isn't a confirmed bachelor who has suddenly decided that he wants company. He is completely happy and content in the fellowship of the Trinity. So happy that he wants to share his life with us. So content that he doesn't need to.

God's word of command is simple and brief: "You shall not eat of the tree of the knowledge of good and evil." He sets up for the man one rule for being in relationship with him. Obeying this word is the way to say yes to him and to his offer of life and love.

That's the tension that we're left with at the end of Genesis 2. A rule has been given, a test of appetite. Will the man pass the test? Will his appetite for God be greater than his appetite for the one thing that he can't have?

The purpose of hunger in our lives is the same. Will our hunger lead us *to* God or away from him?

God's Plan to Feed Us

When God gives this command to the man, he is offering him something that he hasn't offered the animals: a two-way relationship of love. He invites the man to respond to love with love.

God not only made us, he made us for himself. That's the point of the first two chapters of Genesis. Our relationship with him is what is meant to feed our souls. Everything that we long for—including our longing to know ourselves—is meant to be found in a dynamic two-way relationship with the God who made us and knows us.

This is the deep answer to our deep hunger. It's also the written testimony of Christian thinkers throughout the centuries. The African bishop Augustine of Hippo wrote these words in the fourth century: "You made us for yourself and our hearts find no peace until they rest in you."[8] His words still resonate with the hungry today.

But to enjoy that relationship, the man must pass the test.

HUNGER CORRUPTED

Soon after God creates Eve, another character enters the story—a talking serpent. Where does he come from? We're told that he's one of the creatures that God has made. The only other thing that we're told is that he's crafty, a description that is confirmed as soon as speaks.

The Serpent addresses the woman, not the man, and his words question God's words ("Did God actually say . . . ?"). He stirs her doubts about them, and then he flat-out contradicts them. He opposes God's "You shall surely die" with his "You will *not* surely die" (Gen. 3:4).

Which word will the woman believe?

We can all picture the cartoon gimmick of an angel on one shoulder and a devil on the other. They argue their case back and forth while we look from one to the other until our heads start to spin. The devil then throws the angel a final insult, which makes the angel give a self-righteous sniff and disappear. *Poof!* Then we make our choice.

That's what temptation can feel like: an argument between internal voices. But this scene is shaped by an *external* word—the real word given by God to govern not just the man and woman's choices but their very desires.

Which word will the woman act on? She'll choose the one that she wants more. The words of the Serpent lodge in her heart and stir her hunger. The forbidden fruit promises to give her something that God has denied her. Something good—very

8. Augustine, *Confessions,* trans. R. S. Pine-Coffin (New York: Penguin Classics, 1961), 21.

good. To be like God. Never mind that God has already created the man and the woman to be like him, for that is what it means to be made in his image (Gen. 1:27).

The Serpent has made the fruit from the tree sound new and exciting.

The words of the Serpent also insinuate slander against the character of God. "God knows . . ." implies that God has given his command not with their best interests at heart, but with his. It sounds like he's making empty threats just to keep the goodies for himself. "He's not good—he's a liar and a miser" is the Serpent's hiss.

The temptation begins to take hold of the woman's appetite. Not only her senses—what she hears, sees, smells, and eventually touches—are engaged but also her desire. "The tree was to be desired to make one wise" (Gen. 3:6).

Hunger tempted isn't hunger gone wrong. Not yet. Temptation resisted would have preserved hunger as the good thing that God had created. But then the woman made her choice. She and the man both did.

She took the fruit, ate it, and gave some to the man. He ate it. They chose what they loved more, spurning the love of God and preferring to love themselves.

With that choice, hunger went terribly wrong, and with it went everything else.

HUNGER CURSED

Ever since the day of Adam's choice, the lie of the Serpent has lodged in our hearts: *God is not good. His commands are unreasonable. He must be holding back on us.* Now that the relationship has been broken, why should we care about the rules?

We've all had the experience of reducing God to the angel on our right shoulder who argues with the devil on our left.

When we get tired of the back-and-forth wrestling with our conscience, we dismiss them both with a *poof* and go off to do what we want.

I win, we're tempted to think. *I don't need God's pesky rules anyway. I know what's best for me. I certainly know what I want, and what I want right now is not God, but this thing in front of me.*

The problem is that when hunger goes wrong, it breaks the boundaries of normal appetite. Take our hunger to know ourselves. It has become a craving. That's why we endlessly take personality tests and gift inventories. That's why we repeatedly pick up books that promise to tell us about ourselves and put magazines in our shopping carts that offer to help us to understand what color we should wear or why clutter bothers us so.

Once unleashed, our hunger becomes a wild inner beast that rages and demands constant attention. Not knowing ourselves, we become obsessed with ourselves. We turn every conversation into a competition so that we can reassure ourselves that we're winners. Or, if we can't win, we decide not to climb that ladder and instead go off to find a different one, telling ourselves that we may not be great but at least we're good at something.

Or we curl up and quit.

Hunger unleashed becomes hunger insatiable. It threatens to swallow us whole. This is hunger fallen. This is hunger cursed.

They shall be wasted with hunger. (Deut. 32:24)

Through want and hard hunger
 they gnaw the dry ground by night in waste and desolation;
they pick saltwort and the leaves of bushes,
 and the roots of the broom tree for their food. (Job 30:3–4)

You shall eat, but not be satisfied,
and there shall be hunger within you. (Mic. 6:14)

This is death by hunger. And we've brought it on ourselves.

HUNGER RESCUED

It's a good thing that God doesn't go away when we dismiss him. He's not like the cartoon angel on our shoulder: small, petty, and easily dealt with. And that's good news, because he doesn't leave us alone in our misery.

God came to the garden on the day that Adam and Eve blew it for all of us. He came while they were still reeling from their choice, cowering in the bushes, hiding and blaming and naked and so ashamed.

His coming terrified them. *He must be coming to judge us.* So they hid. *He must be coming to kill us. How will we die?* In their minds, that was the only question still left unanswered.

He came, and he called, "Where are you?" The God who knows everything invited their response, calling for them like a father calls for his children when they've stayed out too long after dark.

The man and the woman came out of hiding. God questioned them, asking them to tell him what he already knew. They squirmed and blamed and made excuses. The Serpent was there too, waiting for the scene to play out like he hoped. Waiting for God to follow his own rules and kill the creatures he'd made.

Then God surprised us all.

Curse, Death, and Promise

God turned to the three of them—the man, the woman, and the Serpent—with a curse in his hand and flung it with all his power at the Serpent alone. *"Because you have done this, cursed are you . . ."* (Gen. 3:14). The remaining curses were directed not at the man and the woman personally but at the life they would lead from then on.

Yes, life. Life would continue, though it would be hard and hungry. Life would continue for now, though death would come later. But *life* would continue. The woman would have children. The man would grow food.

What about the death that had been promised? Who then would die? This was important. God had said that whoever ate of the tree would surely die, and the Serpent had said that they would not. If God's Word is to be believed and counted on, it must be true all the time.

God gave the man and the woman not one but two deaths that day—one to be executed immediately, the other promised for some future date. That very day an animal (maybe several) died at God's own hand. He used the animal skins to clothe the man and the woman. The animals died instead of Adam and Eve, covering not just their nakedness but also their true guilt and their felt shame.

The second death came in the form of an announcement of a future event. Death would fall on the Serpent. God promised that there would be a day when the Serpent would be crushed by a descendent of the woman. "I will put enmity between you and the woman, and between your offspring and her offspring; he shall bruise your head, and you shall bruise his heel" (Gen. 3:15).

Far from being a fable to explain why women don't like snakes, this promise points to the end of evil by predicting the death of the Evil One. Evil won't win. There's hope.

And so we leave the garden, devastated but comforted. We came with a question: *Why am I hungry?* We leave with an answer. *My hunger is created by God, broken by sin, and redeemable.*

We can't fix our hunger, but we are given the promise of someone who can.

The Hungry God

Who is up to this challenge? Adam and Eve represent us all. Who can win what Adam has lost? Who can rescue not just us but also our hunger?

John's gospel gives us a clue. "*In the beginning,*" John writes, taking us back to Genesis 1:1, when God was alone on an empty stage—except there was no stage yet. And then John tells us plainly what was only hinted at before: "In the beginning was the Word, and the Word was with God, and the Word was God" (John 1:1). This is a strange sentence. But in a flash of insight, we see why God, even alone, is not lonely. The Word of God is with God and at the same time *is* God. Mind blowing.

Then the stage is created, furnished with scenery, filled with action as the first players make their entrances. The play has barely begun when the plot spins seemingly out of control. The stage becomes crowded, littered with death and debris, as the drama twists and writhes forward.

Enter a new character. In John's words, "the Word became flesh and dwelt among us, and we have seen his glory, glory as of the only Son from the Father, full of grace and truth" (John 1:14).

God the Son—never hungry, always blessed—leaves the director's chair and assumes his place on the stage. The God who is never hungry becomes a baby who cries for milk from his mother. He becomes hungry so that he can rescue our hunger.

The last word won't be *death* but *birth*.

FOR REFLECTION AND DISCUSSION

1. "Managing this hunger doesn't satisfy it" (p. 28). Think about your own hunger for self-confidence or some other desire. How do you try to manage it? Does it work?

2. Review the section "God Made Me to Hunger" and the three sub-points (pp. 32–33). Which of these was the most surprising or meaningful to you? Why?

3. "Will our hunger lead us *to* God or away from him?" (p. 35). Have you ever thought about the purpose of hunger in your life? Identify one area of hunger and think about where it tends to lead you. The prodigal son (Luke 15:17) gives a good illustration of this.

4. Why might the corruption of hunger lead to so many other evils? Consider Proverbs 10:3 and James 4:3.

5. What hope is there for our hunger?

Two

Birth

When I discover who I am, I'll be free.
—*Ralph Ellison,* Invisible Man

*The mind is such a vast, unknown cosmos you can never
even know yourself by yourself. . . . Your appetites are
so infinite you can never satisfy them on your own.*
—*David Brooks,* The Road to Character

When our youngest daughter went to college, she decided that the move gave her the perfect chance to make some changes in her life. No one knew her there. She could start fresh, redefine herself, and become a whole new person.

Rebecca started by changing her name. She dropped her first name—which over time had morphed into Becca, Bexter, Becs, and Becca-Boo—for her more sophisticated middle name, Jane.

Jane. It was the perfect new name for an English major who aspired to study abroad at Oxford. No longer would our daughter be pegged as the runt of the family who wore round glasses to match her round face and who gawked whenever she spilled her milk instead of running for a towel like her practical older sister. No. She would be elegant, refined, deep, kin to Jane

Austen and Jane Eyre and every other Jane she had ever read a book by or about.

She informed us of her plan as we drove her up for freshman week. On our way from the car to the welcome table, she shot us a glance and hissed under her breath, "Now, don't forget. It's Jane! Not Becca."

We were glad that she had reminded us. Some habits are hard to break.

"Last name?"

"Lauterbach."

"Yes . . . here it is. You must be Rebecca." The student volunteer looked up with a smile.

"Actually, it's Jane. Jane Lauterbach."

"Oh. Sorry about that. Someone must have messed up. I'll make sure they correct it."

"Thanks." She flashed us a Becca smile over her shoulder.

Mission accomplished.

A WHOLE NEW ME

We're always trying to reinvent ourselves. I remember my own launch into the college years, leaving the South for the wilds of the far Northeast. I was sure my southern accent would charm those Yankees. But within days I realized that they weren't falling all over themselves to carry my books for me. No, they treated me like I wasn't quite all there—like I should have stayed home in the cotton fields, barefoot and pregnant, where I belonged.

So, as I walked past a trash can one day, I dropped my southern accent into it. Done.

What's My Brand?

The problem with reinventing ourselves is that we don't know what we want. When I told one of my young friends that I was writing a book, she said, "That's so cool. You're reinventing yourself. I wish I knew what I really wanted to do—what my passion is. I guess I'll just keep teaching Pilates until I figure that out."

Changing my name, changing my accent, changing my job. I try on new identities like clothes. I want to rebrand myself but can't settle on the final product. What label does the public want? What packaging will make me satisfied with the person inside?

We want the *Good Housekeeping* seal of approval, the gluten-free, organic, non-GMO symbol that will tell us and everyone else that we are fine, just fine.

So we constantly define ourselves by all sorts of labels, from job titles to food tastes. We chatter with our friends, "I'm an accountant" or "I'm a people person" or "I'm such a chocoholic!" Our announcements bring on a volley of noisy affirmations or contradictions from the others at the table.

Our quieter friends smile and ponder their own preferences. They know that appetite is like a mineshaft, dropping quickly from the surface to the depths. They follow it downward, looking for self-understanding.

But if our hunger is broken, as chapter 1 argued, it will prove unreliable as an internal guide. Our hunger will lead us on a wild goose chase, then dump us before we find our prey. It's no wonder that reinventing myself seems like an endless quest. Suddenly I look around at the identities that I've discarded and feel disgusted by the whole thing.

I'm done with searching for a label. I need a cleanse.

Ready for Radical

You know how it feels when you need something radical. A purge. A cleanse. A detox diet. I always feel that way in January after the excesses of the Thanksgiving to Christmas to New

Year's revelry. At that point, I've become numb with rich food and am eating sweets like a zombie. I realize that I have two choices: personally consume the remaining sugar cookies in a trancelike state or shake myself awake and pitch them.

I pinch myself and choose the latter. Out the cookies go. I'm ready for radical because I know the alternative. I want to feel better about myself. It's hard, but by the end of the month the purge has done its work. It has cleansed my palate, and an apple tastes sweet again. For now.

The truth is, I know it's not a once-for-all fix. I detox and then "retox" because my appetite is still broken. I need something deeper than a cleanse.

I need a whole new me.

Fresh and innocent, bright and shiny. Nothing broken, nothing missing, nothing tarnished, nothing spoiled. Not just repaired or reinvented but restored to the best version of me—a version that I can't even quite imagine. Like a baby, but better.

We love babies. They're so new. Their appetite isn't spoiled yet. "Don't let her have a cookie," the new mom says. "I don't want her to even know about sweets." Her little one smacks on a peach with the gusto that you and I reserve for cheesecake. But just wait. She'll eat her first cookie someday, and then she'll struggle like the rest of us.

We need to become like a baby who isn't just born innocent but who stays innocent and grows up. The Bible talks about such a baby, except this infancy doesn't start with our new birth.

THE BIRTH I NEED

Our cleanse starts with the birth of Jesus Christ, the Son of God. That's the birth that we need first.

Chapter 1 ended with the promise that God himself, the one who never hungered, would come into our hungry world to rescue our hunger by defeating evil and the Evil One. How would he do that? Would he swoop down like Superman and use his superpowers to smash the skull of his enemy?

No, he would become a baby who cried when he was hungry, just like us. He would live a hungry life and would do it perfectly, for us. That was the first part of the divine rescue plan.

What was it like for Jesus to be hungry? Did he have preferences? Cravings? Did he get irritable when his blood sugar was low? Or did his divine nature insulate him from the pangs and cravings that we experience? Did hunger's temptations bead up and roll off him like oil on Teflon? Did he fight off temptation with one hand tied behind his back, not even breaking a sweat?

The Scriptures sketch the outlines of Jesus' humanity:

- When Jesus came to earth, "though he was in the form of God" (Phil. 2:6), he "emptied himself . . . being born in the likeness of men" (Phil. 2:7). He became like us.
- He became like us because "he had to be made like his brothers in every respect" (Heb. 2:17), including our struggles with hunger.
- "Because he himself has suffered when tempted, he is able to help those who are being tempted" (Heb. 2:18). He not only was tempted but also suffered when he was tempted, just as we do.

We can fill in the details of this outline with scenes from the four Gospels and with analogies from our own lives.

You see, we need the God-baby to have real hunger and to really be tempted by hunger and really feel how hard it is. But we also need him not to fail. We need him to pass the test of hunger that Adam, and everyone since Adam, has failed.

We need him to fight until he wins.

Eggplant or Figs?

Jesus got hungry, just as we do. One morning he was walking into Jerusalem from a nearby town, and "he became hungry" (Matt. 21:18). If you've ever taken a long walk before breakfast, you know what that hunger feels like. He needed to eat. It wasn't just an act when he went over to a fig tree to look for fruit.

As a baby, Jesus had to learn to eat. Mary had to introduce solid foods to him when he was old enough. He would have liked some foods better than others. He might have spit out eggplant the first time he tried it and loved figs instead. He might have asked for them on his birthday.

He would have had preferences like us, but he wouldn't have sinned in those preferences—not because he wasn't tempted, but because we needed him to be perfect. If he sinned, his mission would fail. He would be under the curse just like us.

So if Joseph asked him to finish his dinner, Jesus would have obeyed him, even if there was eggplant on his plate. If Mary asked him to share his figs with his brother, he would have done so, even if his brother had just punched him. Even though he loved figs, he wouldn't have binged on them. He might have been tempted to, but he would have fought until he won.

The Bible doesn't give us these details, but we can infer Jesus' victory in situations that mirror the struggles of our lives, because he lived a truly human life.

Perfect Appetite

Jesus had a perfect appetite lived out in daily choices. This included not just physical hunger but the hungers of his soul. How did he manage that? By choosing daily to do the will of his Father, even when it was hard, even when his actions shocked his friends and broke the rules of his day.

That was what he did on the day he sat by a village well at noontime, parched and weary (John 4:4–34). He saw the Samaritan woman who came with her jar. The rules of his day said, "Don't talk to her. She's a woman, an outsider, a sinner." But those rules were not the voice of his Father. Jesus knew why she had come to the well at high noon, and he knew why he was there too. So he began to talk with her, offering living water to her thirsty soul.

When his returning disciples saw Jesus talking to the woman, they shook their heads but kept quiet. After she left, they spoke up, bringing out the food that they'd gotten in town and urging him to eat some of it. That's when he said, "My food is to do the will of him who sent me and to accomplish his work" (John 4:34).

That didn't mean that Jesus wasn't going to eat lunch; it meant that his soul was satisfied by obedience to God because obedience keeps the door of relationship open. This was the satisfaction that God had offered Adam and Eve in the garden. Jesus passed the test that they had failed, not just that day but every day of his earthly life.

On the night that Jesus was betrayed, he faced his most terrible test: obedience to the point of death. Did he face it easily, without emotion or struggle? No, he poured out his prayers in agony. In the end, he submitted to his Father even his hunger for life: "Abba, Father, all things are possible for you. Remove this cup from me. Yet not what I will, but what you will" (Mark 14:36).

He did it for us. He did it so that he could hand us his healthy spiritual appetite in exchange for our fleshly cravings. His perfect life for our broken one.

What Adam Lost, Jesus Gained

Because Jesus passed the test that Adam had failed, he reclaimed what Adam had lost:

- his knowledge of God
- his knowledge of himself
- his sense of God's approval

Adam had lost a close personal relationship with God. He no longer walked and talked with God in the perfect world of the garden. He no longer knew God in the face-to-face way for which he had been created.

But Jesus did. He walked and talked with his Father every day of his earthly life. The disciples were astonished when they heard him pray. He talked with God as if he knew him personally. He did. He knew God not just as God the Son, living forever in "the happy land of the Trinity,"[1] but as God become man, living on earth in a land of thorns and tears.

Adam had suffered a loss of self-knowledge, using fig leaves to hide from God, Eve, and himself. By contrast, Jesus showed a secure self-knowledge throughout his earthly life.

Movies about Jesus often show him struggling with self-doubt about his identity and mission. In the movie *The Last Temptation of Christ* (1988), Jesus is portrayed as torn between his desire to settle down and have a family like other men and the messianic task that seems to come from God. We assume that Jesus felt conflicted, imposing our self-doubt on him because we can't imagine human life any other way.

But the Bible shows us a Jesus who is utterly confident in his identity and calling. As early as age twelve, he knows who he is. He travels with his family to Jerusalem to celebrate the Passover, but, on the return trip to Galilee, his parents suddenly realize that he's missing. In panic they double back to Jerusalem and search frantically, finally finding him in the temple.

Jesus is unperturbed. "Why were you looking for me? Did you not know that I must be in my Father's house?" (Luke 2:49). Twelve-year-old Jesus knows his real Father and has found his

---

1. Fred Sanders, *The Deep Things of God: How the Trinity Changes Everything* (Wheaton, IL: Crossway, 2010), 62.

true home. His finite mind has come to know in real time what his infinite mind knew already.

Jesus' self-knowledge and his knowledge of God were always connected, just as they are meant to be in our lives. Jesus understood his own desires—which we so often don't—and he embraced the will of his Father. Doing his Father's will was food to him (John 4:34).

Adam had lost the approval of God when he was banished from the garden. Ever since, we have all lived east of Eden, wondering if God is mad at us or if he even cares.

But Jesus not only knew himself, he approved of himself because he lived under the full approval of his Father. As a child, as an adolescent, as a carpenter's apprentice, as the head of the household when Joseph died, Jesus always did what pleased God the Father. He lived under his Father's smile.

On the day Jesus entered public ministry, the Father made his approval public: "You are my beloved Son; with you I am well pleased" (Luke 3:22).

Knowing God, knowing ourselves, knowing that God loves us and is utterly pleased with us—Adam lost these things, and Jesus gained them. Our deepest hungers can now be satisfied.

But how will these gains be transferred to us?

A NECESSARY BIRTH

The birth that I need first is Jesus' birth. But to receive his benefits, I need another birth: my own.

A man came to Jesus at night (John 3:1–17). He came with a question, though he never got to ask it.

Who was he? This man was very different from the woman who came to the well at high noon. Not only was he a man, he was at the other end of the social spectrum. She remains unnamed, but his name is recorded for us. Nicodemus was a Pharisee, a ruler of the Jews. He was probably elderly, well educated, wealthy, and highly respected, not just as a leader but as a teacher and moral example. He was at the top of his game. She was at the bottom of hers.

In short, she was an outsider to the God of the Bible. He was a privileged insider.

But Nicodemus was like the woman in one way. He came at night; she came in the heat of the day. Both wanted to avoid being seen. They were both afraid of what people might think. Hunger for approval was their common ground.

What did Nicodemus want? Secular people often want to reinvent themselves. Religious people often want to use God to improve themselves. It seems that Nicodemus was one of the latter, using God for his own purposes. He speaks as if he's presenting the official report: "We know that you are a teacher . . ." (v. 2). He honors Jesus by calling him Rabbi and further compliments him by saying that God must be with him. We wonder what he's going to ask for.

But we don't get to find out. Jesus interrupts him with these words: "Truly, truly, I say to you, unless one is born again he cannot see the kingdom of God" (v. 3).

You're Not In

Whatever Nicodemus's question was, Jesus knew that Nicodemus was assuming one thing. Nicodemus thought he was an insider. He might have wanted to improve his standing in the kingdom of God, but he assumed that he was in. He assumed that he had been born into it because he had been born a Jew. If he needed anything, it was just a few minor adjustments.

Jesus told him, *You're not in. You don't need to be promoted to a higher place in the kingdom—you need to get into the kingdom. Your first birth didn't do it. You need a second birth.*

This statement is a leveler. It means that the homeless woman and the homeschooling mom stand shoulder to shoulder before God. It means that the beach bum who steals the surfboard and the hardworking woman who saved to buy it are on level ground. It means that the sweetest little old lady and the lowlife who knocks her down for her purse have something in common.

A radical restart is necessary for all of us.

Birth Happens

Born again. Nicodemus didn't understand it. We're perplexed by this term too. We know what it means to be born a first time. That is the very definition of a fresh start. We can see that new birth might be a useful analogy for turning over a new leaf, but we can't quite picture it.

"Okay, whatever," we might say. "Birth, reinvent, whatever label you want. What do I need to do to make it happen?"

If we're already asking how to be born, we haven't understood what rebirth is. The point is, we can't do it. We can't give birth to ourselves. This would be ridiculous in the physical world, and it's equally impossible in the spiritual world. Birth is always initiated by the parents, not by the child.

Jesus goes on to give clues to what he is talking about. First, *born again* can also be translated "born from above." This points to a heavenly Father instead of an earthly one: his Father. Second, Jesus says that Nicodemus must be born of "water and the Spirit" (v. 5). Water refers to cleansing. The Spirit refers to God's Spirit, who was powerfully present at the birth of the world and is also the power behind the birth of the believer.

These are the elements so far: (1) the Father's will and (2) the Spirit's power—Jesus hasn't yet talked about his role. The result: a clean new me.

New York pastor Timothy Keller puts it this way: "New birth is an action of God in which his Holy Spirit (his life, strength, power) is implanted in the base of your heart so that the root of your heart is transformed."[2]

"Fine," we might say. "Fine and dandy. But how? If *I* can't make it happen, how in the world is this rebirth supposed to happen?"

Nicodemus asked the same question: "How can these things be?" (v. 9).

Birth by Death

Jesus explains that the new birth is the reason that he came to earth. He came to tell us about it and to make it possible. By way of explanation, he reminds Nicodemus of an episode from Jewish history when many people were dying from the bites of venomous snakes (Num. 21:4–9). Nicodemus would have remembered it well from his studies.

This episode represented yet another case of hunger gone wrong. The people were furious at God and erupted in rebellion against Moses. Their chief complaint was about the food. God sent snakes as judgment. But as soon as the people admitted that they were wrong to rebel, Moses prayed for them and God provided a way—a most unusual way—for them to be saved from the snakebites.

God told Moses to make a snake out of bronze, put it on a pole, and lift it up where everyone could see it. All the people had to do to be healed was look at the snake. Just look.

They couldn't fix themselves. They had to look to God. They had to look at the remedy that God provided.

Jesus made the connection for Nicodemus with these words: "As Moses lifted up the serpent in the wilderness, so must the Son of Man be lifted up, that whoever believes in him may have eternal life" (John 3:14–15). We can imagine him explaining further: "You see, Nicodemus, I'm like the bronze snake hanging

---

2. Timothy Keller, "The New Self" (sermon, *The Gospel of John Part 1*, Redeemer Presbyterian Church, New York City, December 2, 1990).

on the pole. I'm the salvation that God has provided for you. You want to be born again? Look as I am 'lifted up' and believe."

The term *lifted up* was a euphemism of that day for crucifixion. Criminals were "lifted up" when they were crucified for crimes that deserved the most terrible punishment of the time. They had to lie down to be nailed to the piece of wood, but it wasn't until the cross was stood up on its end—lifted up—that the slow dying began.

Why would Jesus need to die like that? We've already seen that he lived a perfect life, right down to his appetite. He didn't deserve punishment at all, much less the severest kind of execution. But he came to rescue both our hunger and us. To do that, he had to not only live our obedience but also take our judgment.

As Jesus willingly hung on the cross for us, God placed all our sins on him and punished him in our place. He placed on him every hunger gone wrong, of body and of soul. Every craving for something bad. Every obsessive desire for something good. Every one of them was paid for. Forever.

Jesus was born so that he could die. He died so that you could be born.

All that you have to do is look at him, believing that he did all this for you. When you do, God takes your broken life and buries it. Then he hands you a new life, the perfect life of Jesus, to be yours forever. God is the one who makes you new. All you need to do is look up and believe.

Birth by Love

There's one more question to ask. Why would Jesus bother? Why was he willing to pay such a high cost so that you and I could be born?

Everyone knows that birth is costly. We come into this world through the pain and blood of another. Someone else paid the cost of your birth. Nausea and heartburn were some of the early installments; groaning labor one of the last.

In a cursed and broken world, childbirth is hard. Some mothers die.

Why would people keep having children? Love. At its best, birth begins in the love of the parents for each other and their expectant love for their child. But even at its worst, in a cursed and broken world of barrenness and rape and unwanted pregnancy and reluctant adoption goodbyes, there is love.

When the baby is laid in a mother's arms, she forgets the anguish for the joy.

Why would God do it? Why would he lay down his life for our birth? He did it for love. One of the most famous verses in the Bible is something that Jesus spoke that day to Nicodemus: "For God so loved the world, that he gave his only Son, that whoever believes in him should not perish but have eternal life" (v. 16).

The Father sent his Son because he loved us so much that he was willing to part with his Beloved. The Son hung on the cross because he loved us so much that he was willing to pay the price of our birth.

The prophets put the same concept in different terms. They pointed past the pain of Jesus' childbearing to his satisfaction, his joy. The cost was worth it. "Out of the anguish of his soul he shall see and be satisfied" (Isa. 53:11).

When we're laid in his arms, Jesus replaces the anguish with joy.

THE NEW ME

Because of Jesus, I'm completely new. It's the perfect reinventing of myself. I'm utterly clean. It's the ultimate cleanse. I have a whole new me—fresh and innocent, bright and shiny, nothing missing, nothing tarnished, nothing spoiled. I am a new creation.

But there's more. My new birth isn't just about me—it's about my relationship with God. The relationship that was broken in

Eden has been restored. The new bond, forged by the blood of Christ, is now unbreakable.

That means that my insatiable hunger to know myself, name myself, and approve of myself can be satisfied because I now have a face-to-face relationship with the one who made me. I can quit hunting for a better name, because I'm not just known: I'm loved. That's how my daughter's quest for a new identity ended. She fiddled with her name until she met a man who loved her no matter what she was called.

In God's presence I'll find myself not just known but named, rescued, and delighted in. God offers this reassurance to his children as often as we need it. In fact, he did this with me recently.

Known

Sometimes I don't get myself. I was trying to wrap up this chapter before a weekend trip. I was almost done, but the ending wasn't quite right, so I asked my husband to take a look.

His advice rang true, but following it would take more work than I'd bargained for. "Thanks," I snatched the pages from his hand, "but I hope it doesn't take long. I just want to be done before tomorrow!"

It did take long. And I wasn't done. Before I knew it, I was throwing a little temper tantrum. It wasn't pretty. *What's up with this? Why am I so upset?* I kept trying to get ahold of myself, but my self refused to cooperate.

The next morning, I was calmer but still confused, so I dumped the whole mess in God's lap. "Help me to sort this, Father." In his presence I began to see what had happened. Along the way, "thy will be done" had morphed into "my will had better get done, now!" It had happened as subtly as shifting my weight from one foot to the other.

I didn't know that this had happened, but God did. He knows me, and he was helping me to know myself.

Named

That moment of self-awareness could have left me feeling guilty. After all, a hunger for my own will had gone wrong and caused problems. God helped me to name the problem and take responsibility for it, but he didn't stop there. He also named me.

My child. Don't trust your plan. Trust me.

My Father wasn't chiding me; he was rescuing me. Nothing had changed. I still hadn't finished the chapter, but I was amazed at the quietness that was restored to my soul. I was able to go off on my trip lighthearted, even though I took work with me. It didn't feel like a problem anymore. My Father was with me.

Rescued

I don't like needing to be rescued all the time. I prefer to think of myself as someone who has her act together, thank you very much. But here I was, busted again.

My ego wasn't going to like this.

Suddenly, instead of loathing myself and resolving to get it right the next time, I began laughing out loud. This was the stuff I had just been writing about! What I had written about Jesus' perfect hunger to do God's will, every time he was tempted to do his own will and didn't, was true. And his perfect hunger was mine right then. I was flooded with gratitude.

In my mind's eye, I held up my tantrum and all the stuff that had led up to it. I imagined God taking it from me, then placing Jesus' beautiful obedience in my now-empty hands.

Rescued, again. And glad, so glad.

Delighted In

Sometimes I wonder if God doesn't roll his eyes when I get myself into trouble again. I picture him stuck in a relationship that he'd like to get out of, but duty calls him to roll up his sleeves anyway.

Fortunately, the very morning of my tantrum, I read this verse in my Bible: "He brought me out into a broad place; he rescued me, because he delighted in me" (Ps. 18:19).

Delighted? Yes, he delights in me. In you. In each of his children. The kind of delight that makes a dad toss his giggling one-year-old into the air and catch him over and over and over. The kind of delight that makes a mom reach for her camera to capture her three-year-old spinning in circles at the park. He doesn't begrudge our rescue. It's the reason Jesus came.

We started this chapter realizing, *I need a whole new me.* God provides for our need extravagantly; his answer is the new birth.

Now I'm not just new, I'm his.

FOR REFLECTION AND DISCUSSION

1. Have you ever tried to reinvent yourself? How did it turn out?
2. What was the first part of the divine rescue plan? Why was it important for Jesus to be truly hungry and truly tempted?
3. What did Adam lose that Jesus regained for us? Which restored loss means the most to you today?
4. "A radical restart is necessary for all of us" (p. 53). Compare Nicodemus to the Samaritan woman (John 3:1–17; John 4:4–34). Despite their differences, what do they both need? What does Jesus offer to each of them?
5. "Now I'm not just new, I'm his" (see above). How is the new birth better than you realized?

Three

Wilderness

*The wilderness holds answers to more questions
than we have yet learned to ask.*
—*Nancy Wynne Newhall*

In January 1987 my husband and I loaded up the kids and moved from Ohio to Arizona. It was a dramatic change. Not only did we put away our winter clothes, but the constant blue sky and plentiful palm trees made us feel like we were on vacation for the first six months. Yes, we may have been in the desert, but this desert came with swimming pools.

A few years later, my husband and I decided to hike the Grand Canyon. We had three months to get ready, and Tucson had plenty of trails. One day we headed toward the Santa Catalina Mountains, pulled our car off the road, and started climbing. The path felt like it went straight up.

We scrambled along the first ascent on our hands and feet, slipping on the gravel. Farther ahead, the trail turned to sharp rock. We were glad we'd sprung for good hiking boots. Tennis shoes couldn't have handled it.

The dry air and steep climb meant that we drained our water

bottles more quickly than we'd planned. By the time we turned back, we realized that we were going to run out.

The sun was high when we sat down to assess the situation. We were out of water with two miles to go—two miles of treacherous downhill hiking. I had a headache. My husband was starting to feel dizzy. We couldn't stay put—there was no shade to hide in, no water nearby. But we were afraid to move on, to deplete our bodies with every step.

A hiker came up the hill.

"You guys don't look so good."

We told him our situation. He reached into his backpack and pulled out two bottles. "Here. I've got more than enough." He climbed on.

I looked down at the bottle in my hands. Perrier. Sweet.

We drove home that day with a new respect for the desert. Its wilderness was not to be trifled with.

THE WILDERNESS

This chapter is about the wilderness. The wilderness is a place of need—of hunger as well as thirst. It's a place where our baseline spiritual hunger seems to increase. It's also a place with no visible means of support. But, surprisingly, the wilderness turns out to be the place where we find God.

Before I lived in the desert, I thought the wilderness described in the Bible looked like the Appalachian Trail: plenty of shade, more than enough water, little overnight shelters dotting the way. Websites about the trail advised me to expect plenty of company too (especially during the hiking season), not to mention an abundance of spectacular views. The wilderness experience didn't sound half bad.

But after hiking in the desert, I know better. The wilderness described in the Bible is more like a desert than a forest—a place of scarcity, not abundance; silence, not birdsong; solitude, not companionship. It's a place of snakes and scorpions.

That's exactly how Moses describes it in the fifth book of the Bible, Deuteronomy: "the great and terrifying wilderness, with its fiery serpents and scorpions and thirsty ground where there was no water" (Deut. 8:15).

We've all spent time in the wilderness—maybe not physically, but spiritually. Those are the times when our life seems to dry up, the familiar landmarks disappear, our friends vanish one by one. The wilderness may be brought on by circumstances we can point to—a downward move, an illness, a job loss, the breakup of a marriage—but wilderness can also occur in the absence of specific adversity. We may even bring it on ourselves.[1]

In the wilderness, we become defined by what we lack.

When my husband and I set out on our hike, we knew that we were heading outside, but we hadn't counted on finding ourselves in the wilderness. The wilderness is never our plan.

My Wilderness

Motherhood was a prolonged wilderness for me. My college years had prepared me for a lot of things but not for having my first child. I hadn't done much babysitting during my high school years either. But it couldn't be that hard, could it?

I didn't realize that a newborn hijacks your schedule, takes over your body, and changes the landscape of your world. For me, becoming a mother felt like wandering into a trackless desert.

Everyone said that motherhood would come naturally. I would just know what to do. I would understand my baby's cries. I couldn't mess it up. Every other mom seemed to be adjusting quite well. Not me.

1. See Psalm 107:17–18: "Some were fools through their sinful ways, and because of their iniquities suffered affliction; they loathed any kind of food, and they drew near to the gates of death."

In the haze of those early weeks, when days and nights mixed together and the baby's cries were my only alarm clock, I floundered. I began to grab for help in all sorts of places. My husband pitched in, rocking the baby with one hand, checking out parenting books with the other.

One resource recommended scheduling the baby's feedings. That made sense to us both. After I implemented the new plan, my combination of inexperience and desperation made me cling to it like a life preserver.

At six weeks, I took Rachel to the pediatrician for her checkup. The nurse measured and weighed her. She left the room quickly. Moments later, the doctor walked in.

"Has your baby been growing fussier lately?"

I nodded and told him the story of her increasing fussiness throughout the day and frequent awakening in the night. I was exhausted and baffled. I thought that I had this thing licked. What was the problem now?

"Your baby is failing to thrive. She weighs less than she did when she was born."

I looked at my child and saw for the first time how big her eyes looked in her bony head. As I poured out my tale of structured feedings, maternal anxiety, and decreasing milk supply, I realized that I had been unintentionally starving my baby.

I was devastated. I had tried to get my act together as a mom, but I had failed. My failure felt like a personal wilderness, but it didn't just affect me. I had brought my baby there too.

QUESTIONS IN THE WILDERNESS

The wilderness feels terrible. It feels wrong. It feels dark. How did I get here?

Even asking that question can feel painful. The wilderness itself is a painful place, but my shock at finding myself there makes it worse. This wasn't part of my plan. How did I get here? Was it my fault—some combination of incompetence plus negligence plus selfishness?

Those questions ran through my head during the weeks that followed that doctor visit. I felt like I had failed not only my baby but God. I wondered if he was punishing me.

More questions come. *Was it me, or is someone else responsible?* A teenager finds out that she's pregnant. She's normally a good girl, but this one time she slipped. There are so many other factors at play. Her parents' indifference. Her boyfriend's insistence. Her friends' pressuring. Surely, with this cast of characters, she can't be the only one to blame? It doesn't seem fair.

We go from blaming ourselves to blaming others. And back again.

In the prolonged pain of the wilderness, the questions multiply. How much longer is this going to last? How can you get out of here? This is when you start trying your strategies. You weigh your options, but none of them sound like the perfect fix. You become desperate enough to try anything. You bargain with God. You vacillate. *I'll give up the baby. No. I'll get the abortion.* You try to get on with your life and somehow leave the wilderness behind.

But you end up running from one desert to another.

You feel so alone in the wilderness. "How are you?" a class-mate casually asks; you give the expected reply. "Fine." But the superficial exchange increases your sense of abandonment. Surrounded by crowds, you wonder, *Does anyone see me? Does anyone care?*

I'm hungry to be seen and cared for in the wilderness. Where is God?

The Hand of God

No matter how you get to the wilderness or what questions you ask there, one thing is certain. God is the one who brought you there.

God is the one who brings each of us into the wilderness. He brings the teen who gives birth and the teen who aborts. He brings the barren one and the mother who fails. He brings the one who runs and the one who hides. He brings the believer and the one who is no longer sure. The wilderness may not be our plan, but it is his.

Why does God take us there? To make us hungry. Hunger always humbles us, but it is especially humbling in the wilderness, where food is scarce. We're used to being able to take care of ourselves, and suddenly we can't. God takes us into the wilderness to bring us to the end of ourselves.

That's the purpose of the wilderness. In the same speech of Moses that we quoted earlier, Moses explains it this way: "You shall remember the whole way that the LORD your God has led you these forty years in the wilderness. . . . He humbled you and let you hunger" (Deut. 8:2–3).

Moses speaks these words to the nation of Israel as he reviews the last forty years of their lives, years that they have spent in the wilderness. He reminds them that this wasn't an accident—God led them there. And he is continuing to lead them all the way through it.

Forty years before, God had rescued the Israelites from slavery in Egypt and brought them into the wilderness of the Sinai Peninsula. He knew they weren't ready for the good life yet. Prosperity would tempt them to forget God—to talk like believers but act like atheists. They needed the wilderness because they needed to learn to trust God.

People come to faith in the wilderness because they quit having faith in themselves.

HUNGER IN THE WILDERNESS

The wilderness is God's way of increasing our hunger. Hunger in the wilderness devastates our faith in ourselves. It's there we see the limits of our ability to satisfy our own deepest needs. The wilderness is where God takes us to reveal this. It makes us turn to him for the food that we need. It makes us ready for the food he wants to give us.

In the meantime, we get cranky. Hunger brings out the worst in us. That's part of the wilderness too.

Sin, Suffering, and Silence

I might not have sinned my way into the wilderness, but I definitely sin while I'm there. I complain about the menu; I grumble about the service. I compare my sorry lot to the greener grass of my neighbor. I fend for myself and try to solve my own problems. I start a social media campaign and stir up other malcontents. I demand better treatment and threaten to pack up and leave if I don't get it.

When I finally settle down and recognize my bad behavior, I feel worse than ever. Any hope I had of earning my way out of the wilderness evaporates. I may have assumed that I didn't deserve to come here, but now I'm certain that I deserve to stay. I begin to feel doomed.

The wilderness continues, and my hunger increases. My questions have gone unanswered. Does anyone see my suffering? Does anyone hear my cries? Am I really as invisible as I feel?

The wilderness finally reduces me to silence. I conclude that I no longer have a case to plead, that I've run out of options. All my hopes have turned out to be false. My questions have trailed off into shrugs.

My groans have evaporated into sighs.

Breaking the Silence

Into the silence, God speaks. He calls you and me by name and opens a conversation with us.

God asks us a question, like he asks Hagar, a servant girl in Abraham's household, when he finds her in the wilderness: "Hagar, servant of Sarai, where have you come from and where are you going?" (Gen. 16:8).

God asks us a question, like he asks Sarah, Hagar's mistress,[2] when he finds her in the wilderness of her infertility. She is leaning against the tent wall, eavesdropping on God's conversation with Abraham, but he means the question for her ears. "Why did Sarah laugh and say, 'Shall I indeed bear a child, now that I am old?' Is anything too hard for the Lord?" (Gen. 18:13–14).

God lets us run out of answers, even out of questions, so that he can speak into our silence.

This was the experience of both Hagar, the runaway slave girl, and Sarah, her mistress. The two women could not have been more different. One owned nothing; the other was wealthy. One was an outsider to the God of the Bible; the other had an inside track. One was pregnant; the other remained barren year after year. One ran away; the other retreated into her tent.

Both were in a wilderness. Both felt invisible, unseen, unheard, forgotten.

And to both God spoke. The wilderness had silenced these women to the point at which they were ready to hear. God called them each by name. He saw them, and now they knew it. He saw Hagar by the spring in a small oasis surrounded by a vast desert. He saw Sarah laugh silently behind the tent wall. He heard them, and now they realized it. He heard Hagar's solitary distress.[3] He heard the bitter question in Sarah's heart.[4] They were no longer invisible.

This is the shock and awe of being seen by God.

2. Her name had been changed from Sarai to Sarah in the meantime (Gen. 17:15).
3. "The Lord has listened to your affliction" (Gen. 16:11).
4. "After I am worn out, and my lord is old, shall I have pleasure?" (Gen. 18:12).

But, instead of answering their questions, God asks them a question. He does that to us too, and it usually comes as a surprise. Our questions aren't the right ones, so he redirects the conversation, taking the lead, opening the door.

The common ground these two women shared was the wilderness—and the God who spoke to them there. God takes each of us to the wilderness for the same reason. The place where we fall into silence is the place where he has our full attention.

The place where we expect to find hunger turns out to be the place where we finally find food.

GRACE IN THE WILDERNESS

The wilderness may be a place of hunger, but when God speaks to us there, he makes it a place of grace. That's the point of the sermon that Moses preaches in Deuteronomy 8:2–16.

Grace is the one thing that can make us laugh out loud. It's not just that it's unexpected—it's simply preposterous. Just when you're expecting to have heatstroke, some stranger hands you a Perrier. Just when you've lain down to die in the desert, God tells you to go home and promises that everything will be OK.[5] Just when your last bit of hope evaporates into self-mockery, God tells you that a child is on the way.[6]

Grace seems too good to be true. All you can do is laugh.

What gifts does God want to give us in the wilderness? In his sermon, Moses gives Israel—and us—lessons of grace to prepare the people for life in the good land. He looks back on forty years of wilderness wandering and points out, alongside their suffering, God's grace in things such as:

5. That was how Hagar's wilderness experience concluded (Gen. 16:9–12).
6. That was what God promised Sarah that day, speaking loudly enough for her to hear through the tent (Gen. 18:10–14).

- his daily provisions
- the chance to know ourselves
- the chance to know our God

Why does God give us gifts? Because his purpose in the wilderness is a gracious one. Moses explains, "Take care lest you forget the LORD your God . . . who led you through the great and terrifying wilderness . . . to do you good in the end" (vv. 11–16). He wants to do us good. That's what we're tempted to forget.

When we look back and remember the wilderness, we're not just supposed to remember the suffering, we're supposed to remember God's grace. We're supposed to remember God. This is the "whole way" of the wilderness that Moses talks about: "You shall remember the whole way that the LORD your God has led you these forty years in the wilderness" (v. 2).

Let's remember together.

His Provision

First, Moses tells the people about God's provisions: "He humbled you and let you hunger and fed you" (v. 3). "Your clothing did not wear out on you and your foot did not swell these forty years" (v. 4).

We're used to having our needs met in ordinary ways. When we run out of milk, we swing past a grocery store. We might be able to get to our favorite store, the one that also carries the kind of yogurt we like and that always has blueberries on sale. But even if we are forced to grab milk from our least favorite spot, in any event, we won't go without. In normal life there are lots of options. God provides for us through ordinary means.

Not in the wilderness. There's not a grocery store in sight. No malls either. No bottled water. For that matter, there's no water at all. Terrifying.

We are forced past our habituated dependence on the ordinary and are compelled to cry out for the miraculous. The insomniac cries out for strength despite no sleep. The single mom cries out for double wisdom and double patience. The woman who can't seem to get healthy cries out for a joy that outweighs her suffering.

That's exactly what God provides. Sleep, a spouse, health—these are all good things. They are the normal ways that he provides for us, but they are not necessary. He is. He is the source of our life. He is the Primary Means behind every secondary provision.

The wilderness is the place where we get to see that most clearly.

Knowing Ourselves

We're eager to know the best about ourselves, but we also need to face the worst about ourselves. That is the second gift that God gives us in the wilderness.

Moses explains that God brought the Israelites to wilderness "that he might humble you, testing you to know what was in your heart, whether you would keep his commandments or not" (v. 2).

I think I know myself. During the lonely, early months of motherhood, I often used to visit my neighbor two doors down. I would show up at her door just after my baby woke from her afternoon nap because I wanted some company. She would let me in, even though she was in the middle of fixing dinner for her family of four. I would sit in her kitchen, and we'd visit while she cooked.

I also made my way down to her house when I needed to borrow things. Sugar. Milk. A toy wagon to use as an ice chest. A lawn mower. A tree trimmer.

Right before we moved away, my neighbor and I went out to lunch together. She took that opportunity to tell me how resentful she was of the many favors I'd asked, the things that I'd borrowed and been slow to return, the things that I'd returned in shabby condition.

I was completely caught off guard. I hadn't seen my selfishness, but the wilderness had revealed it. She was right. All I could do was apologize. That moment of painful self-knowledge was God's gift to me. It brought me to my knees.

But that's not the end of the story. Years later, we were shocked to hear that this woman had died suddenly. When we went by to visit her family, the daughter told me that her mom had talked about me frequently and considered me the best friend she had ever had.

I was shocked again, but also flooded with gratitude. The wilderness of motherhood had humbled me and made me lean on God. I hadn't been able to help but share Jesus with my neighbor during those years, and on the day of my apology I had lived the gospel that I had shared.

The wilderness is a place where God helps me to see myself clearly. It's a place of testing. It's a place of failure. It's a place of humbling. I get to know myself in ways that cause me to quit trusting myself and begin crying out to God.

The wilderness is the place where God humbles me so that I actually begin to change.

Knowing God

The third gracious purpose of the wilderness is to know God. Moses explains, "Know then in your heart that, as a man disciplines his son, the LORD your God disciplines you" (v. 5), and he does so "that he might humble you and test you, to do you good in the end" (v. 16).

I not only think I know myself, but I think I know God. It's like I've walked around life since childhood clutching a little suitcase with the word *God* written on the outside. As far back as I can remember, I've believed in God. But if you had opened up the suitcase, you would have found that it contained only a few small rocks and some toys. My God wasn't very big yet, and my beliefs were a jumble of Bible stories and childish wants.

Sarah's God wasn't very big yet either. She saw him as her husband Abraham's God who occasionally threw a bone to her. Abraham was the one who received the promises, who saw God in a vision, who spoke face to face with God on occasion. She was Abraham's sidekick, his tag-along.

God used Sarah's wilderness to make himself big in her life. He called her by name and spoke to her heart. His grace turned her mocking laugh of unbelief into the hilarity of faith. He was her God now too.

In the wilderness, God empties our small suitcase of childish toys and begins to fill it with solid truth about him. We come to see the painful isolation as necessary preparation for his revelation. We find that the enormous emptiness of the desert is the only platter large enough to serve his abundance.

It's in the wilderness that we begin to look past our failures and see God's faithfulness. It's there that we spy a purposeful hand of discipline in the trackless wasteland. It's there that we learn to call him not just God but Father.

Weighted with this revelation, our suitcase becomes too heavy for us to lift. No matter. He carries us.

Grace in My Wilderness

My wilderness of motherhood deepened before God led me out of it. I gradually adjusted to the humiliation of putting my baby on formula, despite the cries of the lactation police who surrounded me. She began to put on weight and soon delighted us with her first smiles.

To ensure continued weight gain, I was instructed to wake my daughter every three hours during the night if she didn't waken on her own. My husband took his turn now that she was on the bottle. I trained myself to listen for her cry, while counting on the alarm clock to provide backup in case I missed her. I checked the time often in the night, calculating how much she'd eaten as well as how much I'd slept.

Finally, Rachel's weight approached normal for her age, and I no longer had to wake her up. She began to awaken only twice a night and then only once. About the time she started sleeping well, I started having trouble sleeping. I would lie in bed wide-eyed and think that I heard her crying. She wasn't.

At bedtime I was exhausted but not drowsy. I'd toss in my bed, then get up to read for a while before going back to try again. Once. Twice. Sometimes more. I began to fear going to bed at night.

Of course I prayed. I cried out to God. And then I just cried, sometimes in anger. God had promised to take care of me, and he wasn't doing a very good job! I read Scripture in snatches, looking for comfort, a verse that would send me off into dreams. But the wilderness continued, and over time my "quick fix" approach began to change.

I began to realize that I needed more than answers. I needed God to speak. I needed to know him. I began to tell him my deepest fears, and he began to speak to them.

"Father, I'm afraid of my fears. Just when I start to relax and drift off, a ping of anxiety awakens me. I can't control it!"

Child, I can. I am greater than your heart.[7] *Fear not.*

"Father, I'm afraid of tomorrow. How will I make it through the day?"

Child, you are weak, but I am strong. I will give you my grace. It will be enough.[8]

"Father, what am I going to do? You made me to need sleep. How can I live?"

---

7. See 1 John 3:20.
8. See 2 Corinthians 12:9.

Child, I did make you to need sleep, but don't be afraid. You do not live by sleep alone, but by every word that comes from my mouth.[9] *I will sustain you. I know what you need. You need me.*

God led me into the wilderness and made me hungry so that he could feed me with lavish gifts. He sustained me. He caused me to face my fears and to really change. He assured me again and again that I was his beloved child and that he wasn't going anywhere.

And he finally led me out.

GOD IN THE WILDERNESS

When God finally leads us out of the wilderness, shouldn't that be the end of the story? Our hunger is fed, our questions answered. Let's get out of here. But before we move on, there's one more question that we may not have thought to ask.

Where did all this grace come from?

My behavior in the wilderness is never pretty. That's why I tend to assume that my suffering there is some kind of punishment. I keep trying to get my act together so that God will let me out of the time-out chair. *How did I do, Lord? Have I learned the lesson yet? Does this count?*

I figure that I have to earn my way out of the wilderness.

Instead, when I least expect it, long before I even *find* my act, much less get it together, God loads me with gifts and opens the exit door.

What? Who paid for that? And when?

Led, Hungry, Tested

It started on the day when God led God into the wilderness. "Jesus was led up by the Spirit into the wilderness to be tempted by the devil" (Matt. 4:1).

9. See Deuteronomy 8:3.

Jesus had just been baptized. He had just received the full blessing and approval of his Father. God had said these words for all to hear: "This is my beloved Son, with whom I am well pleased" (Matt. 3:17). Then God led him into the wilderness of Judea. This was not a mistake; this was the plan.

Why? Surely Jesus already knew God well enough. He must have known that God would provide for him. Surely he already knew himself well enough. He didn't need the wilderness to test him. Why did God take him there? What would his time in the wilderness accomplish?

God took God there to hunger. "After fasting forty days and forty nights, he was hungry" (Matt. 4:2). Hunger is humbling. It tests us. Adam was tested by hunger in a garden, and he failed. Jesus was tested by hunger in the wilderness, and he passed.

God took God there to be tempted. "The tempter came and said to him . . ." (Matt. 4:3). Jesus faced the same temptations in his wilderness that we face in ours: the temptation to save ourselves, the temptation to test God's love for us, the temptation to grab God's gifts for ourselves. Jesus faced each one of these, not just theoretically, but in real time from a real tempter. The Tempter. The one from the garden. The one who knew precisely how to tempt this victim—with Scripture.

And Jesus didn't fail. He passed each test with flying colors.

God led God into the wilderness for us. He led him there to pass the test of the wilderness perfectly, so that when we failed, we wouldn't get the F that we earned, but the A that Jesus earned for us. That's grace, free for us because it was paid for by someone else.

God led God into the wilderness for our comfort, too. Jesus came to know our suffering there firsthand, so he could help us. Although we feel abandoned, we're really not. "Because he himself has suffered when tempted, he is able to help those who are being tempted" (Heb. 2:18).

But that's not all.

Forsaken

There came a day when God deserted God in the wilderness. On the cross, Jesus entered the most desolate wilderness of all. On the cross, he took our sins on his body and paid the price for every one of them. The small ones that we barely recognize. The big ones that plague our conscience. Our sins in the wilderness. Our sins in the good land.

And on the cross, God poured out the punishment on Jesus that we deserved. The Father turned his back on the Son. The Son cried, "My God, my God, why have you forsaken me?" (Matt. 27:46).

God abandoned God in that wilderness so that he could be God with us in our wilderness.

We've seen that the wilderness brings us hunger, questions. *I'm hungry to be seen and cared for in the wilderness. Where is God?*

Jesus entered the wilderness to bring us answers. *He is my Emmanuel here.*

FOR REFLECTION AND DISCUSSION

1. Are you in a wilderness right now? If not, recall a time when you were. What facts and feelings make it a wilderness for you?

2. Has your wilderness experience undermined your self-reliance? How?

3. We compared the wilderness stories of Hagar and Sarah. Which woman do you identify with more? How did God meet them in their wilderness? Watch for him in yours.

4. According to Deuteronomy 8, what three things does God give us in the wilderness? Can you identify similar gifts in your own experience?

5. How does Jesus' wilderness suffering and victory encourage you today?

Four

Food

The young lions suffer want and hunger,
but those who seek the LORD *lack no good thing.*
—*Psalm 34:10*

Have you ever watched a baby try a new food?

At first she pushes it out of her mouth because she hasn't gotten the hang of using her tongue yet. Then the texture hits her. Her eyes get big, and the gag reflex threatens to put an end to the meal.

If she can get past that, she starts to taste the stuff. She squints and sucks and rolls it around in her mouth. She puckers and purses her lips. A dozen expressions pass over her face while the jury deliberates. Suddenly her mouth pops open for the next spoonful.

It seems that eating is a learned behavior.

My husband and I flew across the country to watch our grandchildren so that their parents could get away for a few days. The baby, Abi, was proving to be a picky eater. Our daughter had left a short list of foods that she liked and a long list of ones that she wouldn't touch. This kid didn't even like bananas.

"Here are a few things I haven't tried yet, Mom. Good luck," she said as she and her husband ducked out the door.

Dinnertime came, and we rolled up our sleeves. I took charge of the older two children while my husband put a bib on the baby and snapped her into the high chair. Yogurt was practically the only thing Abi was enthusiastic about, so he started with that. While he shoveled spoonful after spoonful into her mouth, he perused the list of new foods.

"I think we should try beets. They're sweeter than squash and not as thick as peas."

"Sure." I was busy refilling the plates of the other two, who seemed to like everything.

"Oh, honey, you gotta see this."

I turned around to catch the rolling geography of Abi's face—the furrows and wrinkles and bulges and hollows—as she tasted her first bite of beets. Then she swallowed. My husband slid another spoonful in. Then another and another.

"She likes it!" He grinned happily at me.

He turned back to resume his mission. Right then Abi exploded, spewing her entire helping of beets right into his face, all over his hair, and onto his shirt.

I guess if eating is a learned behavior, we should expect messes.

FOOD, GLORIOUS FOOD

It's time to talk about food. Everyone else is. From food blogs to food truck tweets to food shows to celebrity chef competitions, food is one of our society's favorite topics. And it doesn't stop at our border either. It seems to be a global celebration, multiculturalism at its best.

I have to admit that it's pretty wonderful—both the food and all the food talk. When I wanted to make tacos for some friends who love Mexican food, I searched and found a taqueria-type taco recipe on a food truck blog. Our friends said that it was the best carne asada taco they had ever tasted. When I needed a dessert idea for a bridal shower, I checked some baking blogs for inspiration. The pictures alone were worth my time, but beyond that was the chummy, don't-you-wish-I-lived-next-door-to-you commentary. I felt like I'd made a new friend.

Yes, food is glorious. But it also can become a problem. It's not just a celebration—it's a preoccupation for most of us, even an obsession. I know. I've been there.

The Problem of Food

I didn't start having issues with food until my mid-teens. That summer I went away to work as a camp counselor, working up an appetite and working my way through lots of good and not-so-good camp food. I'd always been able to eat whatever I wanted, but I didn't know that things had changed. My body had stopped growing, and my appetite hadn't heard the news.

When I arrived home, my then boyfriend greeted me with an affectionate, "Hi there, butterball." I growled at him. But when I checked myself out in front of the mirror, I saw that he was right. I'd gotten chubby.

I began trying to lose the weight, checking the mirror and scales weekly, then daily, then hourly. Before long I found myself trying many of the unhealthy eating behaviors that characterize 50 percent of teenaged girls[1] today—things like skipping meals, making drastic restrictions, even fasting. I would push my food around at the dinner table or make an excuse to skip dinner entirely. After a few days of that kind of behavior, I would end up binging on anything I could get my

1. These behaviors also characterize 30 percent of teenaged boys. See Dianne Neumark-Sztainer, *"I'm, Like, SO Fat!"* (New York: Guilford, 2005), 5, cited in "Eating Disorder Statistics & Research," *Eating Disorder Hope*, accessed May 25, 2015, http://www.eatingdisorderhope.com/information/statistics-studies.

hands on. Every Monday I would start over with new rules and fresh resolve; by the weekend I would have blown my plan completely.

Food became a problem for me. It was my favorite love-hate relationship. I thought about it all the time—what I could eat, what I couldn't, when I could eat, and when I didn't dare. It was like an addiction, except I couldn't deal with the substance by going off it cold turkey. That would have made it so much easier. But since I had to eat, it seemed that the problem of food wouldn't go away.

If only I could find the perfect food.

The Perfect Food

What is the perfect food? That's a question that gets lots of Internet space these days. The answer to it depends on who you're asking.

To a foodie, the perfect food might be anything with bacon. If you're talking about the most balanced nutrition in a single food, many people insist that the egg is your answer. If you're looking to add perfect to a not-so-perfect diet, you can choose from a range of probiotic, spirulina-enriched, antioxidant, healthy carb, green juice supplements. There's even a peanut butter nutrition bar that calls itself *Perfect*. (I happen to agree with that one.)

Why do we want to find the perfect food? Because food is a problem, and we want a solution. We want something that will be tasty but not addictive. We want something that will stabilize our blood sugar, make us strong, clear our brain fog, and increase our energy. We want something that will satisfy us instead of leaving us craving more. We want to feel perfect, look perfect, be perfect.

We're hungry for the perfect food that will delight and satisfy us without tempting us.

Food Perfectionism

Unfortunately, we don't do perfect well, which means that the quest for perfect often leads to trouble. Even if the perfect food could be found, we would have to develop perfect rules for eating it. Then we would have to follow those rules perfectly. Before long, we would leave the path of normal living and head into the wasteland of perfectionism. This is the terrain of eating disorders, where food brings death instead of life.

My own diet struggles didn't go that far, but author and blogger Emma Scrivener's did. She writes vulnerably about her anorexia—not just how it happened, but how it felt. Her quest for perfect masked a quest for control. It was all about the rules—her rules. "With my body, I was able to create my own universe. A realm where I ruled, with unquestioned sovereignty. I was no longer at the mercy of my feelings. I was in charge: a self-created, stainless-steel person. Bleached to perfection."[2]

Emma found that she could rule her intake of food, but the result wasn't health, life, or satisfaction. Self-rule reduced her. It drove her past human limits into animal starvation. She determined to control herself at all costs, even up to the cold perfection of death.

Her struggles continued for over a decade, through illness, diagnosis, recovery, and relapse. In the end she met God in a way that she hadn't met him in her previous encounters with Christianity. Emma explains her transforming encounter: "I wasn't in charge—but I'd met the One who was. The God who could satisfy all of my longings and all of my hunger. Before him, I could hand over control and not be destroyed. He was enough, and he wanted me."[3]

2. Emma Scrivener, *A New Name: Grace and Healing for Anorexia* (Downers Grove, IL: InterVarsity Press, 2012), Kindle edition, chap. 3.
3. Ibid., chap. 8.

Only God can do perfect perfectly. It turns out that he both designed the perfect food and sent it from the sky.

FOOD IN THE WILDERNESS, PART 1

In our last chapter, we learned about hunger in the wilderness. We learned that God brings the outsider and the insider into the wilderness to increase our hunger for the food he wants to give us. What is his idea of the perfect food?

At this point, our story intersects with the story of Israel, God's people, in the wilderness. Let's pick up the thread in Exodus 16. God has just delivered the people from slavery in Egypt through the birth canal of the Red Sea into the desert of the Sinai Peninsula. It's been six weeks since their miraculous birth, and they're no longer cooing. They're wailing for food.[4]

The Problem of Food

A baby's cries can set your nerves on edge. "Use your words," a mom tells her fussy two-year-old. Imagine the sound of this mob of angry adults. It wasn't pretty. "The whole congregation of the people of Israel grumbled against Moses and Aaron in the wilderness" (Ex. 16:2).

The problem of food was simple: there wasn't any. The people's hunger was legitimate; their need was real.

What should they do about it?

It's obvious to us. They should remember clearly, ask nicely, and say thank you. They should remember the ten rounds of escalating miracles they had seen God do, with the parting of the Red Sea as an encore. Surely food wouldn't be a problem for this God. The Israelites weren't on speaking terms with him yet, but Moses and Aaron were, so all they had to do was ask

---

4. The complete story of this incident is found in Exodus 16:1–20.

them to ask God. Based on God's past faithfulness, they should probably have started setting the table.

This process is called *reasoning by faith*. It was faith because the people still had to look to God for something that they couldn't provide, but it was reasonable because of God's track record.

Instead, the Israelites put both faith and reason on hold and had a temper tantrum. In one breath they said the equivalent of, "I wish I were dead. . . . Why are you trying to kill me?" First they wished that God had killed them back in the good old days when they were slaves with full stomachs. Then they blamed Moses and Aaron for their predicament, as if the exodus had been a maniacal plan dreamed up by those two.

The situation was laughable, unless you were Moses and Aaron. They had a right to be indignant with such a ridiculously false charge laid against them. It was pathetic, unless you were God. He had a right to be offended by their insult to his saving power. Their cranky complaints against Moses and Aaron were really complaints against him.

What would God do to them?

The Gift of Food

God would feed them. That's grace. God didn't even wait for Moses and Aaron to approach him. He started the conversation, telling them his plan: "Behold, I am about to rain bread from heaven for you" (Ex. 16:4). He wasn't rolling up his sleeves to hurl a lightning bolt at the Israelites; he was rolling up his sleeves to make breakfast.[5] Bread from heaven. Who saw that coming?

5. There were times that God disciplined the people for their crying and craving (see Numbers 11:4, 31–35), but grace tempered his judgment. The last word on the wildernesses is not their failure but his faithfulness to his own promises (see, for example, the words of Psalm 105:42–43: "For he remembered his holy promise, and Abraham, his servant. So he brought his people out with joy, his chosen ones with singing").

With the food came rules—God's rules for gathering, preparing, and eating this bread. These were the right kind of rules about food, like instructions on the outside of the packaging written by the chef himself. You would be a fool to ignore them.

The rules were meant to guide their food prep, but they had another, more important function. They were meant to test God's people. Would they take his words seriously? Would they follow his rules precisely? Would they eat his food his way?

The next day God made good on his word—bread came like rain. The morning dew came as usual, but when it evaporated, there was some flaky stuff left that looked like frost. "What is it?" The people didn't know what to call it or what it was for. It was a new thing.

Moses had to tell the people what it was. "That stuff is the bread." Then, since it hadn't hit the food blogs yet, he had to tell them what to do with it. They could bake or boil it, and it tasted kind of like honey on crackers—food, glorious food. They dubbed it *manna*, which meant "what is it?" because they still couldn't relate it to anything they'd eaten before.

God gave his babies food, a perfect food, a strange food. Eating it would be a learned behavior.

THE MEANING OF THE MANNA

The food never ran out. God planned to feed his people from his own kitchen for as long as they needed it, as long as they were in the wilderness. When two years turned into forty because of their disobedience, he didn't run out of supplies. And he didn't hold out on them either. Manna continued to be a daily gift from his own hand.

Forty years later, Moses recounted their wilderness history.

At that time, he explained the meaning of the bread that rained from heaven.

Strange Food

We've already spent some time in the sermon that Moses preached in Deuteronomy 8. In our last chapter, we learned from it that God uses our hunger in the wilderness to increase our appetite for his food. Our new birth, the topic of chapter 2, begins this new appetite.

The food that God sent the Israelites was manna, but beyond filling their stomachs, it served as God's pivotal visual aid for another kind of food—his Word: "He humbled you and let you hunger and fed you with manna, which you did not know, nor did your fathers know, that he might make you know that man does not live by bread alone, but man lives by every word that comes from the mouth of the LORD" (Deut. 8:3).

The bread from heaven had been strange food to these people forty years before. They had needed to learn to eat it. But bread wasn't the only food that God had given them. The manna had been accompanied by the words of God: instructions about gathering and not gathering, storing and not storing.

Just as their stomachs needed bread, their souls needed God's Word. So God fed them with his very words, given from his mouth to their hungry souls, like a mother bird hovering over the hungry mouths of her young.

This, too, is strange food. Who ever heard of feeding on words, especially words from one who is invisible? It must be a learned behavior.

Living on every word that comes from the mouth of God isn't something that comes naturally to us. Have you ever felt that way? We have to learn to do it, not just with the tools of a good Bible study but in the training ground of the wilderness.

That's where we realize that God's words are our perfect food.

Perfect Food

How can God's words be the perfect food for each of us? Don't we all have different needs? The outsider might find inspiration from some of his words but reject others as outdated or just plain wrong. The insider has favorites too. Maybe God's words are like a buffet, where I can pick and choose the ones that I have a taste for. I don't care for sushi, so I'll gravitate toward the pastas and salads before I pick out my sweet treat. How nice of God to provide such an assortment!

But God's words aren't a buffet table of options. Every word from his mouth is meant for us. "All Scripture is breathed out by God" (2 Tim. 3:16).

That's because God doesn't speak throwaway words like we do, careless comments tossed out there on a whim. Every word of his is purposeful.

- His word makes things happen. "Let there be light" (Gen. 1:3).
- His word is true. "The rules of the LORD are true" (Ps. 19:9).
- His word draws lines. "He assigned to the sea its limit, so that the waters might not transgress his command" (Prov. 8:29).
- His word is a precision instrument. "For the word of God is living and active . . . discerning the thoughts and intentions of the heart" (Heb. 4:12).
- His word is eternal. "The grass withers, and the flower falls, but the word of the Lord remains forever" (1 Peter 1:24–25).

Some parts of the Bible are sweet to our taste. They're the ones that show up on refrigerator magnets and greeting cards. Some parts are salty or bitter. They're the ones that challenge our worldview or guilty pleasures. Some parts are just plain hard to comprehend. They're the ones that lie outside the boundaries of our present experience or understanding.

When the outsider goes from indifferent to hungry, the Bible is the place for her to turn. When the insider goes from hungry to indifferent, the Bible is still the balanced diet that she needs. This Word is for everyone.

FOOD IN THE WILDERNESS, PART 2

There was just one problem with the manna. The people got tired of it. There was just one problem with the command to "live by every word that comes from the mouth of God." They couldn't do it.

We have the same problem when we apply the lesson of Deuteronomy 8:3 to our Bible reading plan. We get tired of the Book. And we don't do so well at believing the promises or obeying the commands, either. The food might be perfect, but we aren't.

At about this time, our eating disorders kick in. We fast from disobedience, then inevitably we binge again. We put ourselves on a healthy eating plan of Bible reading, and then we blow our diet, pigging out on social media instead. We grovel in shame and make more resolutions to try harder.

Perfectionism comes into play. Some of us try to come up with perfect rules for eating this perfect food. One woman told me, "I eat three physical meals a day, so I figure the least I can do is read my Bible three times a day. So, before I allow myself to eat breakfast, I have to read my Bible."

Oh dear. We need help. And God is going to take us to another wilderness to give it.

The Problem of Food

This other wilderness was also filled with a crowd of hungry people and scarcely any food. In the famous story of Jesus' feeding a large crowd from a little boy's lunch, even the numbers are well known. Starting with five loaves and two fish, Jesus fed five thousand families and still ended up with twelve baskets of leftovers. Not only that, but it's the only miracle that Jesus did that is recorded in all four Gospels (Matt. 14:13–21; Mark 6:32–44; Luke 9:10–17; John 6:1–13).

But why is this story so important? What does it mean?

Just like in Exodus 16, the problem of food was simple—there wasn't any. Jesus and his disciples had chosen to go to a desolate place because they were trying to get away from the crowds. They had been so busy that they hadn't had a chance to eat. They themselves were hungry and needed a break.

But the crowds had followed them. Imagine the disciples' dismay when they looked up and saw a mob trudging up the hill toward them. Five thousand men and their families. It was a sea of need.

Their hunger wasn't just physical. They had been tracking Jesus around the countryside "because they saw the signs that he was doing on the sick" (John 6:2). They could have been hungry to see another miracle or hungry for their own healing or hungry to find out what the sign was pointing to.

In a crowd that size, multiple hungers were at play. What matters is that Jesus took their hunger seriously. He saw that they were like "sheep without a shepherd" (Mark 6:34). He knew that their hunger was real and that they had no resources of body or soul to meet it. He didn't see them as a problem, like the disciples did. He didn't wish that they would go away and leave him alone.

Instead, he had compassion on them. And he already had a plan to feed them.

The Gift of Food

The food was a gift. Jesus didn't owe the crowds a meal. He could have sent them away in good conscience. This was Galilee, not the desert of Sinai. There were villages nearby.

Feeding that many people would be an expensive proposition. That was the disciples' worry. They couldn't imagine bankrupting the treasury so that this mob could be satisfied. They did a quick mental calculation and realized that the appetites in front of them completely exceeded their ability to pay. They were quite fretful over the whole situation.

Not Jesus. As a perfect man, he reasoned by faith. *God the Father fed the people in the wilderness for forty years. This picnic is well within his capacity. The only thing left to do is ask and give thanks.* So he took the loaves and gave thanks, his faith providing the precise solution to Israel's faithlessness hundreds of years earlier. That day, his perfect obedience earned the grace that God gave to his people in Exodus 16.

Then, as incarnate God, Jesus himself multiplied the bread without show or effort.

He made it look so easy. As if it didn't cost him anything. All that abundance, plus the leftovers, without breaking a sweat. The crowd knew it was a sign. But they didn't realize what it pointed to. For them it was another trick by the miracle-working prophet. Many of them would come back the next day for an encore. "Do it again!" they'd cry like children who can't get enough.

They had no idea what it would cost him.

THE MEANING OF THE BREAD

John is the only gospel writer who explains the miracle.

When the crowds returned the next day, Jesus connected the dots for them. "More bread please," they started, but since yesterday's miracle reminded them of the manna, they couched their request in biblical terms: "Our fathers ate the manna in the wilderness" (John 6:31), so . . . more bread, *please!*

Jesus said that they were on the right track but the wrong train. "Truly, truly, I say to you, it was not Moses who gave you the bread from heaven, but my Father gives you the true bread from heaven" (v. 32). Manna was once again a visual aid, a sign pointing to something else.

Okay, fine, they agreed. *Then that's what we want. Give us the true bread. We'll work for it if we have to.*

That's when Jesus told them what the sign pointed to. Him. "I am the bread of life; whoever comes to me shall not hunger, and whoever believes in me shall never thirst" (v. 35).

Strange Sermon

The conversation gets complicated and goes long. At some point, Jesus comes to the synagogue and preaches a sermon. I'll summarize his three main points.

Bread from heaven is pure gift. "My Father gives you the true bread from heaven" (v. 32).

Literal bread is only partially a gift. Rain comes down and waters the fields, but you must plant and harvest and grind and bake bread. God's part is the rain—that's pure gift. The rest is up to you and your work. Your normal food is a cooperative effort between you and God.

But bread from heaven is different. It's pure gift. You don't have to plant, harvest, grind, or bake it. That's why I'm telling you that "my Father gives you the true bread from heaven. . . . I am the bread from heaven" (vv. 32, 35).

I am the gift.

I am the one who does all the work. I came down to do the work—all of it. I came down to do the will of God by living perfectly (v. 38), by living according to every word that comes from the mouth of God. I came down to do the will of God by dying in your place (v. 51). I came down to do the will of God by earning life and giving it to everyone who looks and believes (v. 40).

The work is finished. There's no work left for you to do.

All you need to do is eat. I'm handing you my life like a loaf of bread. Your job is to take and eat. You are to feed on my finished work. To consume me. The only way I can get my life into you is to be broken like bread. It will cost me everything. But I do it for you.

Strange Food

That was his sermon, sort of. I cleaned it up. Jesus was more graphic: "Whoever feeds on my flesh and drinks my blood has eternal life. . . . For my flesh is true food, and my blood is true drink" (vv. 54–55).

The people were offended by his words. They understood animal sacrifice for sin, but these words were over the top. Never had they eaten raw meat. Never had they drunk blood. Never had a person been sacrificed for them. They drew back. Many left.

The cross of Christ is offensive. It is terrible in its torturous physical suffering. It is terrifying in the outpouring of judgment it represents. We shrink back from the blood and wrath.

But the real offense of the cross is to our pride. I want to make my contribution, however small. I want to work for my food—and to feed on my work. I gag on grace.

Feeding on the finished work of Christ is a learned behavior. God has to bring me to an end of my if-I-try-harder-I'll-eventually-get-it life. He pushes me until I'm really out of options. He takes me into the wilderness to feed me with Christ.

When I'm broken, his broken body is the food I want. I begin to get a taste for grace.

Perfect Food

Remember where we began this chapter?
We're hungry for the perfect food that will delight and satisfy us without tempting us.

Jesus is our True Bread. Feeding on him means feeding on his finished work for us—his perfect obedience and atoning sacrifice.

We do this whenever we take the bread and drink from the cup at the Lord's Supper. This is more than remembering; this is feeding. The sacrament is a visual aid, much like the manna. It makes Jesus' sacrifice tangible to our senses. The bread is soft between our fingers. The cup gives off a sweet smell as we bring it to our lips.

It's also a sign, much like the manna, pointing beyond the symbols to the reality that they signify. We watch as the pastor tears the loaf in two. Jesus' body, broken for me.

Jesus is also the True Word that we are meant to live by. We're meant to feed on his finished work in our Bibles.

His perfect obedience turns all the hard sayings—commands that we break and promises that we fail to believe—into good news. "Do this, and you will live" (Luke 10:28) becomes "I've done this so that you can live." His atoning death turns all the sweet sayings into lasting comfort. They tell us, "I love you because I love you, even to the point of death on a cross."

Jesus is our perfect food. His perfection is the end of our perfectionism.

FOR REFLECTION AND DISCUSSION

1. Have you ever tried to find the perfect food or diet? What happened?
2. Compare God's gift of manna to Israel (Ex. 16) with his gift of food to Adam and Eve (Gen. 1–2). What can this teach us about God's character?
3. The manna points to God's Word as our food. How has the Bible seemed like strange food to you? Like food that you needed to learn to eat? Like perfect food?

4. When we hear that "man lives by every word that comes from the mouth of the LORD" (Deut. 8:3), we immediately think of the Bible. But how does that statement ultimately point to Jesus in his life and death?

5. "Jesus is our perfect food. His perfection is the end of our perfectionism" (p. 94). Ponder this statement for your own life. Turn your thoughts into a prayer.

Five

Craving

Something unappeased, unappeasable is within me.
—Friedrich Nietzsche, Thus Spoke Zarathustra

But they had a wanton craving in the wilderness,
and put God to the test in the desert.
—Psalm 106:14

I hate it when I do this.

Tuesday is my long day at work. Since I don't get home until seven o'clock, I usually try to put something in the slow cooker before I leave the house. But today I overslept. I figure I can throw together some fried rice with the leftovers from last night's dinner. That will be quick.

On the drive home, I remember that there is a half-eaten bag of tortilla chips in the pantry. They are my favorite kind too—ones that I recently discovered in the snack aisle. They're light and very crisp, with just the right amount of salt.

I'll have a few of those to tide me over before I make dinner.

My husband arrives home moments after I've pulled the leftovers out of the refrigerator and found the recipe.

"When's dinner?"

"Soon."

"Need help?"

"Nope." I don't want to share the tortilla chips with him.

I grab the bag as soon as he leaves the room. *I wonder if there's any leftover salsa in the refrigerator.*

Half an hour later, my husband wanders into the kitchen. By then I've polished off the bag of chips and cleaned up the evidence. I feel kind of gross. I jam the rice into the microwave and begin savagely chopping an onion.

"How much longer?"

"Just a couple of minutes. There should be plenty for you. I'm not very hungry."

I hate it when I spoil my appetite with junk food.

NOT SO PERFECT FOOD

We've all done it—let our cravings get the best of us, overdosed on junk food when real food was only minutes away. We mean to have just a few. We know better. But it tastes so good, and we can't stop.

Let's face it. The food we need isn't always the food we want. And the food we want often spoils our appetite for the food we need.

When we finish our binge, we come out of it with no one to blame but ourselves. Not only have we ruined our appetite, but we also feel awful. Women may say, "I feel gross." I've never heard a man say that. We curse our lack of self-control and make resolutions about next time.

We usually binge on things that aren't bad in themselves. We don't often grab for some heroin or snack on cyanide. It's food we want, reasonably good food—we just eat too much of it or reach for it at the wrong time.

Cravings are an everyday problem for most of us, spiritually as well as physically. Spiritual cravings can sidetrack us from feeding on the food that we need—the perfect food that we learned about in the last chapter: Jesus.

Junk Food for the Soul

We tend to wake up hungry—and not just for breakfast either. Some mornings we know what we're hungry for. After a frustrating day, you may be hungry to get a lot accomplished that morning. After a fight with your husband, you may wake up hungry to make things right with him.

Other days you and I aren't sure what we're hungry for. *I feel so restless today, bored, tired of the same old stuff.* I wander around the house, see the same chores waiting for me—the broken lamp still needing repair, the mess that the dog made on the carpet. Again. The list is endless, and I don't want to deal with it. I want life, adventure, some action, maybe romance.

When I feel this way, sitting down to read my Bible sounds like one more chore. Same old, same old. I check Facebook instead. I snack on Instagram. I dip into Pinterest. I catch up on my favorite blogs. I'm looking for life online, because those words seem to promise a quicker fix than the words of Scripture do.

Social media websites aren't bad in themselves, but they aren't meant to be my daily bread. Treating them that way indulges my cravings while leaving me empty. Feeding on them every time I get the whim creates habits that are hard to break. I begin to lose my freedom to choose and end up being at the mercy of my moods.

Feed Me Another Compliment, Please

When I first started writing, I got an e-mail from an author who I highly respected complimenting my work. I felt exhilarated. I must have read that e-mail several dozen times. I took in every word. I practically memorized it. No, actually, I *did* memorize it. Perfectly. That way I could meditate on it when I wasn't at my computer.

I fed on that e-mail the way I'm supposed to feed on Scripture.

And that e-mail fed me—the parts of me that don't need to be fed. My pride grew. My sense of identity began to lean on it. My happiness sucked life from it. My craving for compliments grew stronger.

What do you feed on when you have a craving? It all depends on what you love. The reason I fed on that compliment was because I love accomplishment. I'm a recovering performance junkie, and a taste of success can make me fall off the wagon.

What do you love?

If you love money and the things it can buy, chances are you turn to the mall or online shopping when you feel the pull of craving.[1] You feed on your latest purchase and the compliments you get when you show it off. "Oh, that dress is so you!" But before long, you've used it up and have to go shopping again. *I've got nothing to wear!*

If you love the feeling of being in love, you may feed on fantasy. You go from real-time crushes to romantic comedies and back again. Texting may become your soul food. You hear the ding, and your heart leaps. If your fantasy life thrives on secrecy, you may download Snapchat or Whisper so that you can share your soul without leaving a trail.

If you love to be right, or at least to pick a good fight, you might feed on controversy.[2] There's plenty of that on the Internet. Your sense of injustice grows stronger as you follow a local or global quarrel. If you've been personally offended, the craving

---

1. The Bible speaks directly to this craving, warning us of its danger. "For the love of money is a root of all kinds of evils. It is through this craving that some have wandered away from the faith and pierced themselves with many pangs" (1 Tim. 6:10).

2. This craving, too, is identified in Scripture. "He has an unhealthy craving for controversy and for quarrels about words, which produce envy, dissension, slander, evil suspicions" (1 Tim. 6:4).

is even more insatiable. You simply can't get enough fuel for your fire.

Do you feed on approval? To-do lists? Adrenaline? Entertainment? We instinctively feed on what we love.

What Happened to My Childlike Appetite?

The Bible invites us to love and to long for God's words like a baby feeding on milk.

> Like newborn infants, long for the pure spiritual milk, that by it you may grow up into salvation—if indeed you have tasted that the Lord is good. (1 Peter 2:2–3)

Pure spiritual milk. This description of God's Word perfectly fits the analogy of the new birth. It captures the radical nature of conversion, the new life that begins with faith in Jesus. Our new life produces an insatiable new hunger for God and his goodness that can be met only by meeting him in the Scriptures.

Why then would those of us who have come to love Jesus turn from our perfect food to spiritual junk food? *Why* these cravings? *How* do they happen? And *what can we do* about them?

WHY? THE ONGOING PROBLEM OF CRAVING

When our craving for the wrong kind of food—both physical and spiritual—is strong, we can get discouraged. We feel like we're back to square one, like nothing has changed. But God's Word says otherwise.

The new birth is a fact for anyone who believes in the life, death, and resurrection of Jesus Christ for her sins. This fact brings with it two permanent, internal changes in the life of a believer. God makes both these changes clear to us through his words to the prophet Ezekiel: "I will give you a new heart, and a new spirit I will put within you" (Ezek. 36:26).

Our new heart is soft and responsive to God, soft enough for him to write his Word there (Jer. 31:33; Heb. 10:16). We have a new desire to know God—everything about him—and to understand what pleases him. What we *should* do and what we *want* to do begin to line up. We begin to experience wholeness—the reintegration of the various parts of ourselves that sin has shattered.

Our new spirit is none other than God's own Spirit, sent to make his home in us. "I will put my Spirit within you, and cause you to walk in my statues and be careful to obey my rules" (Ezek. 36:27). We now have an internal guide who is also our strong ally. We now have both the desire for what is good and the power to choose it.

We now have a new love that trumps all the other loves in our hearts—a love for God, a responsive love for the one who loved us first. That's why the words of Scripture become sweet to us.

We instinctively feed on what we love. *So why do we still feed on junk?*

Leftover Junk

Why? Because we still have our old appetite too. And it still craves junk. These cravings are called "evil desires" in the Bible because they are simply desires gone wrong. For example, our desire for significance is meant to be met by God's approval and applause, but we crave it from the people around us instead. Cravings are made of our leftover love for the wrong things. Or for the right things, loved in the wrong way.

Why does God leave us this way? Why doesn't he eradicate our old appetite when he gives us the new? That question is above my pay grade. In God's wisdom, he has begun the radical change that will transform every part of us. He will also complete the work that he began; we can be sure of that.[3] On the day he finishes—when we die or when Christ returns—we will be freed from sinful craving, forever.

But until then we will experience struggle between our two natures and their conflicting appetites. The struggle is real, and it makes us feel a little schizophrenic. Apparently the nineteenth-century poet Edward Sandford Martin felt this way too, because he wrote this poem about it.

> Within my earthly temple there's a crowd:
> There's one of us that's humble, one that's proud;
> There's one that's broken-hearted for his sins,
> There's one who, unrepentant, sits and grins;
> There's one who loves his neighbor as himself,
> And one who cares for naught but fame and pelf.
> From much corroding care I should be free
> If once I could determine which is Me.[4]

We may not understand why God leaves our old appetite in place, but we can be sure that it's not an accident. It's God's plan, so it must be a good one. Here are some possible benefits from our ongoing struggle with cravings:

- *The struggle keeps us dependent.* We cry out for help when our cravings tempt us. "God is faithful," Paul promises, "and he will not let you be tempted beyond your ability, but with the temptation he will also provide the way of escape, that you may be able to endure it" (1 Cor. 10:13). We wonder how he's going to deliver us *this* time. Then we get to see his faithfulness in action, again.

---

3. Paul writes, "I am sure of this, that he who began a good work in you will bring it to completion at the day of Jesus Christ" (Phil. 1:6).

4. Edward Sandford Martin, "Mixed," *Sly Ballades in Harvard China* (Boston: A. Williams and Company, 1882), 5.

- *The struggle unites us with each other.* The cravings that I experience aren't much different from yours.[5] Even if I'm tempted to feed on accomplishment and you prefer nibbling on entertainment, we're still in this together, you and me, because there are no unique temptations. We can help each other. We can pray for each other.
- *The struggle reminds us that God is our only Savior.* This fact, first experienced when we first believe, becomes our ongoing experience during our ongoing struggles. When we give in to our cravings, we feel the need for our Savior. Again. We confess our sins, and he forgives us. Again.[6]
- *The struggle dignifies us by calling us to participate in the fight.* It's flesh against Spirit,[7] and we're called to war, to take up arms against our old self with the weapons of the new self. The Spirit is our ally, the battle forging deeper friendship between us and our indwelling God.

The struggle may be hard, but it gives us a chance to experience the gospel over and over. In God's hand, it feeds our love for the right thing.

HOW? THE PREDICTABLE PATH OF CRAVING

How does craving for the Not So Perfect Food develop? It follows a predictable path. Let's look at it so we'll be better prepared for the fight the next time.

5. "No temptation has overtaken you that is not common to man" (1 Cor. 10:13).

6. "If we confess our sins, he is faithful and just to forgive us our sins and to cleanse us from all unrighteousness" (1 John 1:9).

7. "For the desires of the flesh are against the Spirit, and the desires of the Spirit are against the flesh, for these are opposed to each other, to keep you from doing the things you want to do" (Gal. 5:17).

First, there's an attractive thing[8]—something that gets our attention in the moment. Like the forbidden fruit in Eden, it awakens our emotions and promises happiness. I'm sitting down to read my Bible when I glance over and see the Sunday paper. Suddenly the newspaper is fascinating. The Sunday comics can't wait. The editorial page calls to me. The arts and leisure section sings to me. I'm hooked.

Second, my desires start to pull on the hook. This looks good, and I want it. I have an itch for life, and this will scratch it. I have a longing for love, and this will fill it. I reason. *I can always read my Bible later.* I bargain. *I'll read twice as much later if I look at the paper now.* I'm being dragged by desire.[9]

Third, the Spirit in me begins to resist. *Live by my Word today. Hear it, read it, believe it, live it. I have life to give you. I want to woo you with love. The paper can wait.* The battle begins. Whose side will I join?

This might be a day when I vacillate. *You're right, but . . .* I make excuses. *I'm tired; give me a break.* I whine. *Really? Life? Your Book's not that interesting. I already know how it ends.* I argue.

If this continues, I begin to doubt. *Prove it. Are you really as good as you say? Or are you holding back on me? Are you enough?* I put God on trial. In the wilderness, God tests me, but in my cravings I turn the tables. I test God.

I'm heading toward that moment in the garden. Doubting God's goodness. Ready to reach out and take something that I want more than him.

Fourth and finally, I choose. Craving gives birth to sin.[10] What I choose becomes my god in that moment. I'm saying, "This is my god. This is what I need first and most. This will feed me."

---

8. "So when the woman saw that the tree was good for food, and that it was a delight to the eyes, and that the tree was to be desired to make one wise . . ." (Gen 3:6).

9. "Each person is tempted when he is lured and enticed by his own desire" (James 1:14).

10. "Then desire when it has conceived gives birth to sin" (James 1:15).

The fight against cravings is always a battle against idolatry. What I choose shows what I worship.

WHAT CAN WE DO? THE WAY OUT OF CRAVING

Idolatry? That sounds pretty extreme, you might say. After all, it's only the newspaper!

Idolatry is a serious charge, I agree. It's a violation of the first commandment: "You shall have no other gods before me" (Ex. 20:3). But it's even more than that. The first commandment is not just first; it's foundational. The German reformer Martin Luther pointed this out, asserting that every single act of disobedience—from largest to tiniest—starts with breaking that first commandment.[11] Sin doesn't just break a command; it replaces God.

We're guilty of idolatry more often than we realize. Yikes! The good news is that understanding idolatry can help us to understand our craving and find the way out.

On the Idol Hunt

Before we start talking about idolatry, I have one caution. I don't want to send us off on an endless internal idol hunt. Why might we do that? Because once we see how central idolatry is to our struggle, we want to roll up our sleeves and get to work. We want to fix the problem. But we can't. It's too big for us.

Idols are serious. Idolatry is the first interior step of rebellion that precedes all the other, more visible ones. It's the hidden evil behind every unkind word and self-centered action. It's present in my passive withdrawal from doing good (an idol of comfort) as well as in my active refusal to do it (an idol of self-interest).

---

11. See Martin Luther, *A Treatise on Good Works* (1520; Project Gutenberg, 2008) Part X,

Not only that, but idols abound. The list of things that I place before God is endless. I can be a very nice person and find out that I crave the approval of others. My niceness is a quilted cover-up for my idol of approval. I can be a very hard worker and suddenly realize that I crave achievement. My productivity is the innocent cover sheet for an idolatrous resume.

And that's just the beginning. Once we start the idol hunt, we seem to find them everywhere. It's overwhelming. Self-awareness of our idols can be helpful at first, but if we feel that we have to name every idol before we can be rescued from it, we will panic and start running in circles of endless introspection.

We can't save ourselves from our idols. Only the true God can do that.

The Problem of Idolatry Is the Problem of Love

The problem of idolatry is always a problem of love. What I love most is my god. I feed on what I love: my god, my idol.

Remember my story about feeding on a compliment? I loved how it made me feel. I longed for more of that feeling of love. My longing for love wasn't bad, but I was looking for it in the wrong place. As my pastor preached recently, "The things I'm chasing aren't strong enough to fulfill the desires of my heart—they will break my heart instead."[12]

XI, http://www.gutenberg.org/files/418/418-h/418-h.htm. Speaking about the first commandment, he says, "Now you see for yourself that all those who do not at all times trust God and do not in all their works or sufferings, life and death, trust in His favor, grace and good-will, but seek His favor in other things or in themselves, do not keep this Commandment, and practise real idolatry, even if they were to do the works of all the other Commandments" (Part X). Luther's insight was brought to my attention by Edmund Clowney and Timothy Keller, "Preaching Christ in a Postmodern World" (lecture series, Reformed Theological Seminary, Orlando, FL, 2002), which I accessed online at https://itunes.apple.com/us/itunes-u/preaching-christ-in-postmodern/id378879885?mt=10.

12. David Nutting, "Christianity and Culture" (sermon, *The Gospel Changes Everything*, North City Presbyterian Church, San Diego, CA, July 5, 2015).

He's right. With that compliment, I felt like I had stepped onto the first rung of a ladder that I wanted to climb. At the top was success, happiness, fame, life, love. Or so I thought. But the testimony of those who make it to the top tells another story. Success fails to deliver the unfiltered joy that it promises. It breaks our heart and leaves us jilted.

That's why the Bible unmasks our idols. They are unworthy of our love. They are useless at fulfilling our desires. Paul warns the early Christians to learn from the mistakes of their ancestors in the wilderness. They are on a dead-end path.

"Flee," he says. "Flee idolatry." In love he pleads, "My beloved, flee from idolatry" (1 Cor. 10:14).

But where can I go with my disordered loves? With my broken heart? With my clinging idolatry?

To Jesus.

Fleeing from Idolatry Means Fleeing to Jesus

We need to come to Jesus the way that a rich man did one day (Mark 10:17–22). He came running and knelt down before Jesus, before blurting out the question that was on his mind: "Good Teacher, what must I do to inherit eternal life?" (v. 17).

This man had everything. According to three gospel accounts, he was rich, he was young, and he was a ruler. Not only that, but he was also a law keeper, an insider. But with all those good things—health, wealth, beauty, success—he knew that something was missing. He was dissatisfied. He was reaching for something just out of his grasp.

Jesus talked with him. He challenged his use of the word *good*. He checked on his obedience to the law of God.

But then he did something wonderful. He stopped and looked at him. He saw him for who he was. And the Bible tells us that he "loved him" (v. 21). That's an unusual line in the

Gospels. We know that Jesus loved people, but only a few times does the text say so explicitly.[13]

What did Jesus see that made him love the man? A law keeper? An insider? No, he saw an idolater. He saw a man who had made money his god and didn't even know it. Jesus loved him in his idolatry, while he was still a sinner. He loved him not just by teaching him but by offering to save him.

"You lack one thing; go, sell all that you have and give to the poor, and you will have treasure in heaven; and come, follow me" (v. 21). Jesus was telling him, "Flee idolatry. Flee to me."

The man went away, grieved. The word *grieved* translates to a soul-wrenching feeling that we might have when the dearest thing we have in the world is threatened.[14] We're filled with dread and feel like we're about to die. The man's wealth was indeed his idol. It was the thing he loved most, more than God.

The word meaning "grieved" is used another time in the Gospels. In the garden of Gethsemane, Jesus said, "My soul is very sorrowful, even to death" (Matt. 26:38). What did he dread losing more than anything else? The Father. He knew that the cross would separate him from the Father, and he was in anguish about it.[15]

You see, Jesus wasn't an idolater like the rich young ruler. He loved God his Father, first, most, always, and forever. That's why he challenged the rich man's idolatry. And that's why he said, "Follow me."

Where was Jesus going? To the cross.

If the man had followed, he would have arrived at the foot of the cross, where Jesus, who wasn't an idolater, was suffering

---

13. The other times are John 11:5 and John 13:23.

14. Tim Keller, "Camels and Money" (sermon, *The Hard Sayings of Jesus*, Redeemer Presbyterian Church, New York City, August, 27, 2000).

15. Ibid.

and dying as an idolater. For him. He would have looked up into Jesus' eyes as he hung on the cross and seen the same love that he had seen that day by the road to Jerusalem.

Jesus loves idolaters like you and me. Seeing him love me in this way when I'm in the grip of craving changes me. It breaks me. It makes me gasp at how good he is. It makes me want to love him back.

If idolatry is how we step away from God, worship is how we return.

RESTORED APPETITE

The gospel changes my desires by showing me the one who is most desirable. Coming to Jesus when I'm at my worst is so important. I must not stay away and try to clean myself up first. It's his finished work that atones for my cravings and restores my appetite for him.

Because I have two natures, I need Jesus' saving work to continue while I deal with the cravings that surface all the time. And it does continue. Now that his sacrifice is complete, I'm meant to feed on it by faith in the Word and the sacraments. Now that Jesus has been raised from death, I'm meant to live a new life. Now that he's ascended, I'm meant to count on his prayers and the help of the indwelling Spirit.

But how does this look?

Let's go back to our passage about God's Word being the milk that we need to grow in our salvation, but let's back up one verse to get the whole picture:

> Put away all malice and all deceit and hypocrisy and envy and all slander. Like newborn infants, long for the pure spiritual milk, that by it you may grow up into salvation—if indeed you have tasted that the Lord is good. (1 Peter 2:1–3)

We don't need to be surprised by our cravings. God isn't. This passage assumes the problem of a spoiled appetite—and the answer of the gospel.

- Spiritual cravings can take many forms—but each expresses some failure to love God or our brother. Be on the lookout for them. Malice. Deceit. Hypocrisy. Envy. Slander. They're spoilers.
- "Put them away" points us back to the gospel. The language is of taking off dirty clothes and putting on a new, clean set. It assumes that Jesus has already done the hard work of being born again. Fleeing is one way to "put them away." Fighting is the other way. We do both in dependence on the prayers of Jesus and the power of the Spirit.
- Now our newborn hunger for Christ in the Word is restored.
- The Word feeds our faith. We continue to grow up in God.
- We've tasted God's goodness in the past. It's a familiar taste to us now and a sure sign that our appetite has been restored.

Appetite restored, we are free—free to read the newspaper if we want. There is such sweet freedom in our lives when our loves are properly ordered.

We started this chapter asking, *If I love Jesus, why do I still feed on junk?* The answer to our cravings lies in the gospel.

The finished work of Christ atones for my cravings and restores my appetite for him.

FOR REFLECTION AND DISCUSSION

1. "We instinctively feed on what we love" (p. 101). What kinds of spiritual junk food do you crave?
2. Our ongoing struggle with cravings can be discouraging, but there are benefits as well. Which of the four bulleted

points in the Leftover Junk section encourages you today? Why?

3. "The problem of idolatry is always a problem of love" (p. 107). How can we fix the problem of love? How does the story of the rich young ruler show us the answer?

4. Read 1 Peter 2:1–3. How does verse 1 make verses 2–3 possible?

5. "There is such sweet freedom in our lives when our loves are properly ordered" (p. 111). What does this look like in your life?

Six

Satisfaction

Satisfy us in the morning with your steadfast love,
that we may rejoice and be glad all our days.
—Psalm 90:14

In any and every circumstance, I have learned the secret
of facing plenty and hunger, abundance and need.
—Philippians 4:12

Moving day dawned with a gray drizzle. We were already up, ready to implement our complicated plan. Half of our furniture and moving boxes would go into storage. A few larger items would be donated to a school. The remaining pieces had been measured and chosen to fit the tiny townhouse we had just rented.

We'd moved several times before, so we knew how to do it. But this time was different.

Our previous moves had been upward ones. From an apartment to our first house. From seminary to our first church. From an assistant position to a senior position. The sadness that we felt about leaving one place had always been tempered by our excitement for the next. But not this time.

This time we weren't just moving away. We were moving down.

What had gone wrong? We had moved into this house with high hopes, ready to begin the work that we had been called to do. This city, this church, was where we wanted to pour out our lives and eventually retire. But it seemed that everything we touched went wrong. No sooner was one problem solved than ten others surfaced to fill its place. The harder we worked, the more things fell apart.

As the ministry unraveled, so did our relationships. Conflicts erupted, then hardened into division. People who we thought were friends surprised us. The work began to feel not just hard but lonely. Finally, the end came. It was time to leave.

The day that we moved from our home to the townhouse was so strange. We had no prospects. More than that, we had no friends.

In the past, moving day had always felt like a party. Old friends had come to help us load up. New friends had crowded in to meet their new pastor and help us to unload. Now we had no title, no job. Who would help us this time?

We had come to the city full of hope. We were leaving empty. Would satisfaction ever come?

WILL WE BE SATISFIED?

For five chapters, we have followed the story of hunger in the Bible—a story that is relevant for each of us. This chapter brings us to the end of that story. Where will it end, in frustration or satisfaction? Will we be left empty or full?

We ask these questions because we've all had disappointments in life that have made us heartsick. Wisdom tells us, "Hope deferred makes the heart sick, but a desire fulfilled is a tree of life" (Prov. 13:12). *Desire fulfilled* is none other than hunger satisfied. That observation rings true to our experience.

You may have had your own version of a downward move.

Lingering unemployment emptied your bank account just when you had hoped to buy your first home. A broken marriage ended your hopes for a happy family. Recurring pain sent your heath into a tailspin, reducing your lifestyle to bare existence. Times like these—times of fruitlessness, loneliness, and futility—seem to make a mockery of our hunger for life at its fullest.

Even on our best days, satisfaction is only fleeting. The hard-earned promotion brings a surge of exhilaration. The long-awaited family reunion brings a flood of warm emotion. Of course, the moment of joy fades—we've come to expect that. But even the moment itself seems tinged with fear, marred with regret.

We're always waiting for the other shoe to drop.

Frustrated hopes can make us cynical about the deep hungers of our souls. We can end up lowering our expectations about life until they are almost nonexistent. Deadening our desire feels like the only way to protect ourselves against disappointment.

In a world filled with frustration and fear, what hope do we have of satisfaction? *Where will hunger end?*

The Story of Our Hunger

Let's review our story of hunger so far. We've learned that

- our hunger is good, created by God to be satisfied;
- our hunger was corrupted when the first man and woman ate the forbidden fruit;
- God the Father sent God the Son to rescue our hunger;
- God the Son lived a life of perfect hunger and died for our insatiable, false hungers;
- our new birth in Jesus begins a new, true hunger for God;
- God uses the wilderness in our lives to increase our hunger for God;
- Jesus is the Bread of Life, our perfect food for our true hunger;

- cravings are the leftovers of our old hunger;
- Jesus' finished work atones for our cravings and restores our true hunger.

True hunger. That's one fruit of Jesus' work on the cross for us. True hunger is the healthy appetite that wants God first of all and, after that, every other good thing that he has made for our enjoyment. Things like family. Friends. Work. Rest. Peach cobbler.

The problem comes when those good things don't work out. Circumstances leave us with a mixed message about where our story will end.

Let's say you move to a new city and are hungry for friends. Soon you meet someone who is fascinating and funny and who has the same interests as you—a real kindred spirit. *Satisfaction.* She is a gift from God for the hunger of your heart. Months later, circumstances bring about a perfect storm in your growing friendship, leading to misunderstandings, anger, distance, neglect. A rift forms, then turns into a canyon. *Frustration.*

Our feelings respond to the roller coaster of our circumstances. We feel jerked between joy and sorrow, full and empty. Eventually, our feelings shape themselves into doubts and fears. Two questions emerge.

- Is God really good? (Doubt.)
- Is God mad at me? (Fear.)

Both questions are important. We need to ask them. We need to answer them too, but not from the perspective of our changeable circumstances, not on the basis of our subjective emotions. We need an answer that comes from outside ourselves—from the objective, unchangeable written Word of God. His word about Jesus.

Is God Really Good?

We may be shocked to hear ourselves ask the first question. We know that it comes straight from the garden of Eden, from the dialogue between the Serpent and the woman. Although we may know the doctrinally correct answer to our question, our doubts resonate with it.

Is God really good? If he's as good as he claims to be, then why does it feel as though he's withholding something good from me?

Remember our discussion from chapter 1 about this scene in Genesis 3. God's one command—don't eat from the tree in the middle of the garden—wasn't just an assertion of his right to rule us. It also provided the basis for our relationship with him. The rule was a meeting ground between God and us. God asks, "Will you trust me? Will you love me?" By our obedience, we say, "Yes!"

The Serpent attacked this mutuality, this relationship, through his lies. "God is not good. In fact, he's holding out on you."

Theologian Sinclair Ferguson writes, "The lie was an assault on both God's generosity and his integrity. Neither his character nor his words were to be trusted. This, in fact, is the lie that sinners have believed ever since—the lie of the not-to-be-trusted-because-he-does-not-love-me-false-Father."[1]

Timothy Keller calls this lie a "spiritual poison" that has "passed deeply into us."[2] As a race, we've all been infected by it—every one of us, from the most religious to the least. We shouldn't be surprised when we hear this question surfacing in our souls. The lie lives inside us.

This is why every bitter circumstance brings the taste of this poison to our tongues again. Doubt rumbles most loudly when

---

1. Sinclair B. Ferguson, *The Whole Christ: Legalism, Antinomianism, and Gospel Assurance—Why the Marrow Controversy Still Matters* (Wheaton, IL: Crossway, 2016), 69.

2. Timothy Keller, *Preaching: Communicating Faith in an Age of Skepticism* (New York: Viking, 2015), 53.

our souls feel empty. If God isn't good, we're left with Eve's option: reach out and *take* the goodies for ourselves.

Before we address the answer to this question, let's look at the next one. Though they sound different, they're actually related.

Is God Mad at Me?

If I think that God is holding back on me, I will try to figure out the cause. Either he's not good or I'm not good. The latter option assumes that God must be mad at me. What have I done? What can I do to get back in his favor? Instead of choosing Eve's option (reach out and take), I go with a second option: *earn* his goodies.

Have you ever had a wealthy friend—someone who's not only fabulously rich but also very generous?

Imagine that this friend invites you to stay with him for a week at his vacation home in Maui. "My house is your house," he says with an expansive gesture. And he means it.

You're timid at first, not wanting to overstep your boundaries, but that evening you realize that you forgot your toothbrush. You knock on his door. "I'm so sorry to trouble you, but I seem to have left . . ." He opens a hall closet stocked with supplies and says, "Take anything you need. There's a bathrobe and slippers for you in your room too."

The next morning, you realize that you left your only pair of shoes outside and that they're soaked with rain. Without hesitation, your friend hands you his credit card and the keys to his Jaguar. "There's a Neiman Marcus down the road. They should be able to help you find a pair."

The whole estate is your playground, except for one closet. He keeps it locked.

He pointed it out to you on the first day and told you that it was private. Every time you walk past it, you wonder what's inside. By the middle of the week, your curiosity gets the best of you. *What could be in there? It must be really valuable.* The key is lying on the floor. You check behind you and begin quietly unlocking the door.

"What are you doing?!" His voice makes you jump. "Didn't I tell you that I would give you anything you needed? Why are you breaking into my one locked closet? If you had asked me for anything, even something I keep in there, I would have given it to you!

"You're going to have to leave."

He's mad at you. Why? Because you have not only broken his rule; you have insulted him. In fact, you have rejected him. Your friend's generosity was not an offer simply of his stuff but of himself. Trust breached is also love rejected. He has a right to be angry.

"If you had asked . . . I would have given it to you!" His words are similar to what God told King David after David's terrible sin with Bathsheba. It points to God's astonishing generosity.

David had violated Bathsheba, killed her husband, forced her to be his wife, and then kept silent about it for a year. We're not surprised when God confronts him through his prophet and takes the life of the child he conceived. His response is both justifiable and just.

But God's grace floors us. God forgives David, spares his life, and then, most amazingly, pleads with David to test the boundaries of his goodness: "I anointed you king over Israel, and I delivered you out of the hand of Saul. And I gave you your master's house and your master's wives into your arms and gave you the house of Israel and of Judah. And if this were too little, I would add to you *as much more*" (2 Sam. 12:7–8).

Is God good? The answer to the first question is yes. God is the generous friend who welcomes us into his house with open arms. All our sins come from doubting his goodness. Whenever we try to pry goodies out of what we assume are God's unwilling hands, we insult him. He has a right to be angry.

Is God mad at me? He was.

But not anymore.

THE SATISFIED GOD

God has a right to be angry with me. The real problem behind my satisfaction isn't my changeable circumstances or my yo-yo emotions; it's my fickle faith. My confidence in the goodness of God rises and falls like the tides. I go to bed satisfied and wake up empty.

Do you love me? Are you still good? I know that you helped me yesterday, but what about today?

The Serpent's poison continues to surface in each of us. We treat God like a lazy employee who is on probation. We subject him to daily performance reviews. We question both his competence and his commitment. The poison does its work, just as the Serpent intended. It poisons our relationship with God.

How can God be satisfied with me if I'm always questioning his goodness? If God isn't satisfied with me, what hope do I have of satisfaction?

Believing That God Is Good

What would it look like to believe that God is good, not just sometimes but all the time? It's hard to imagine it, but fortunately we don't have to leave this to our imagination. The pages of the four Gospels put flesh on it for us.

Jesus *believed* that God is good, and he said so. Remember the rich man? When he came up to Jesus to ask him a question, he began, "Good Teacher . . ." Jesus immediately challenged him. "Why do you call me good? No one is good except God alone" (Mark 10:18).

In challenging the rich man, Jesus challenges me. What do I mean by *good*? Honestly, I think of *good* as a weak, small word with a small meaning. Jesus' words remind me of the blazing purity of true goodness. Only God is good. And Jesus believed it.

Jesus also *trusted* God's goodness. When you believe that God is good, you pray. Jesus prayed, and his prayers completely baffled his disciples. They had never heard anyone pray like him. So Jesus taught his disciples to pray by drawing a contrast between them and God. "If you then, who are evil, know how to give good gifts to your children, how much more will your Father who is in heaven give good things to those who ask him!" (Matt. 7:11).

How much more? I get it. I doubt God because I think he's like me, a mix of good and evil. But he's not. He's just good, period.

Jesus believed that. His teaching and prayers prove it.

Acting on God's Goodness

But what about God's actions? When you believe that God is good, you *obey*. Did Jesus live out his belief that God is good?

To answer that, let's go straight to the hardest obedience of Jesus' earthly life. The night before he was crucified, Jesus went to his good Father to ask if he could please be spared from going through with it. "My Father, if it be possible, let this cup pass from me; nevertheless, not as I will, but as you will" (Matt. 26:39).

In his desperation, Jesus asked not once, but three times. He was in agony, both physically and spiritually. Sweat poured off him, tinged red with blood from burst capillaries.

Jesus asked, but the Father said no. So Jesus obeyed. If God is good, then all his words are good. If God is good, then obeying him is good. Jesus believed in the goodness of his Father all the way to the cross. "Being found in human form, he humbled himself by becoming obedient to the point of death, even death on a cross" (Phil. 2:8).

In the first garden, humanity doubted God's goodness and ate the fruit. In this garden, Jesus trusted God's goodness and drank the cup.

Satisfied

What cup is that? It is the cup of God's anger over our disobedience—and not just over our actions but over the continuous slander they imply. The good God is continually slapped by our unbelief. This is the cup we were supposed to drink. He has a right to be angry with us.

But God has no reason to be angry with his Son. Jesus obeyed perfectly. His every obedience affirmed that his Father is good and does good. It vindicated his goodness. His perfect obedience satisfied the Father perfectly.

We needed Jesus' obedience to be perfect obedience. That way he wouldn't store up any of God's anger for himself. But his final obedience was the one we needed most. We needed Jesus to take the cup from us and drink it. On the cross, he drained it completely.

The good Father has been satisfied by the good Son. Jesus' death for our sins has vindicated his Father's justice. Does this sound like heavenly child abuse? Don't picture it that way. This brought them both anguish. The good Father sent the good Son.[3] The good Son laid down his life willingly.[4] This satisfaction was the fruit of love.[5]

Now God is satisfied. Not just with Jesus but with me. Through my faith in Jesus' death, Jesus has taken my penalty and given me his perfect obedience.[6] It's as if I have always—every minute of every day—believed that God is good and acted accordingly. It's as if I always will.

---

3. In the familiar words of John 3:16, "For God so loved the world, that he gave his only Son, that whoever believes in him should not perish but have eternal life."

4. "Greater love has no one than this, that someone lay down his life for his friends" (John 15:13).

5. "In this is *love*, not that we have loved God but that he loved us and sent his Son to be the propitiation for our sins" (1 John 4:10).

6. "For as by the one man's disobedience the many were made sinners, so by the one man's obedience the many will be made righteous" (Rom. 5:19).

This is why God is no longer mad at me—not at all. Jesus drained the cup of God's anger on the cross. There's nothing left for me. Not one drop.

Because God is satisfied with the obedience and sacrifice of his Son, I will be satisfied with his full blessing.[7] That's propitiation.

A satisfied God is my hope for satisfaction.

SATISFIED NOW

God is satisfied with me. I say these words to myself, but I'm not convinced. What do they mean?

God may not be angry with us anymore, but we often feel as though he's not really happy either. We picture God like a dad who tells us to mow the lawn and then points out the spots that we missed. "I guess I'm just going to have to do this myself," he sighs and grabs the mower out of our hands.

We feel as though he tolerates us at best. On our good days, we imagine that we catch him smiling at us occasionally, but on our bad days we picture him frowning behind his newspaper. So we tiptoe past him, hoping we won't tick him off again.

We need to see that God doesn't just tolerate us; he loves us. His love for us in Jesus is as unchanging and personal as his anger was when we were in our sins. When we say that God is satisfied with us because of Jesus, we mean that the relationship has been restored. We're reconciled. He really does love us.

Do these words fall flat? "God loves me?" says one of my teenaged friends. "I'm just not feelin' it."

A Promise of Satisfaction

"Do you love me?" Tevye asks his wife, Golda, in the 1964 musical *Fiddler on the Roof*. She answers him by reviewing all the

---

7. "Blessed are you who are hungry now, for you shall be satisfied" (Luke 6:21).

things she's done for him during twenty-five years of married life. Her actions speak love. She has lived out the promises of their wedding day in the days and minutes of raising a family with him.

This is committed love. It doesn't fluctuate with moods. It's the kind of love that God has for us, the kind that causes him to commit himself to us in Jesus no matter what.

That's wonderful, but what about passionate love? Does God love me with that kind of love too? The kind that pursues, gets jealous, doesn't hold back, gives until it hurts?

Yes. That too is the love that God has for us in Jesus— passionate love that pursues us even at the cost of his own life. He wants us to bank on it, to draw on it when we are struggling with our unsatisfied hungers. We do that by feeding on promises such as this one:

> What then shall we say to these things? If God is for us, who can be against us? He who did not spare his own Son but gave him up for us all, how will he not also with him graciously give us all things? (Rom. 8:31–32)

His passionate, committed love backs up this promise. Love satisfies us while we wait for its fulfillment.

A Prayer for Satisfaction

One psalm in the Bible bears the name of Moses as its author. It contains a prayer that's so helpful when we're struggling with unrequited hungers: "Satisfy us in the morning with your stead-fast love, that we may rejoice and be glad all our days" (Ps. 90:14).

This psalm comes out of the wilderness. Moses himself must have learned to pray it during his forty years there. Think of it. Forty years. That's fourteen thousand six hundred days, give or take.

Picture Moses waking up on, say, day 11,964. He walks out of his tent and looks around him. The sun is just rising. The air is still cool. He hears the stirring of others in their tents. Tousled heads emerge one by one. His sandal hits a rock and sends a lizard skittering into a hole where it will wait out the heat of the day.

What else does he see? Manna. Manna! Not just on day 1 or day 21 or day 461, but today. The manna was a visible sign of God's committed love for his people through forty years in the wilderness. God satisfied their hunger every single morning until they crossed the Jordan into the land that he had promised. Moses prayed that they would eat manna and taste love.

But Moses was also waiting for the final morning, the morning when they wouldn't need the manna anymore.[8]

Manna points to Jesus. Jesus was so determined to make the connection for us that he did the same miracle twice. He fed five thousand one day and four thousand another. Why repeat it? So that we would get the point.[9]

Jesus is our food. His death for our sins turned his body and blood into our life-nourishing food. He is the visible sign of God's passionate love for his people. When we feed on his life and death for us, our souls are satisfied with his steadfast love one day at a time.

So we eat his words and taste the love, but we're waiting too, for the day when faith will become sight.

Moving Downward into His Steadfast Love

During the downward move that I described at the beginning of this chapter, God fed my husband and me with his steadfast love through Scripture in some very specific ways. The first came from the last sermon that we heard before we

---

8. "For he was looking to the reward. . . . He endured as seeing him who is invisible" (Heb. 11:26–27).

9. The point that the disciples failed to get! They fretted over their lack of bread when they were crossing the sea after the second miracle had occurred. Jesus was exasperated. "Do you not remember? . . . Do you not yet understand?" (Mark 8:18, 21).

moved. The text was Jeremiah 29. God's message to Israel—and to us—was that God was sending us and that we were to "seek the welfare of the city where I have sent you into exile, and pray to the LORD on its behalf, for in its welfare you will find your welfare" (Jer. 29:7).

These words helped us to turn outward instead of wallowing in self-pity over our hardship. We were encouraged to picture God's active involvement in our exile and to know that we were right where he wanted us. We also pictured Jesus' descent into exile for us, to seek our welfare. We knew that we were not alone.

God also encouraged us at the end of that trial, as we came to a decision point about what to do next. I was wrestling with some deep doubts and fears as we traveled to check out our options. Suddenly my fears emerged as questions: *What if we do this and you let us down, Lord? Can you really be trusted? Will we be put to shame?*

I remembered that I had memorized words like those in Psalm 25 a few years before, so I flipped there in my Bible.

To you, O LORD, I lift up my soul.
O my God, in you I trust;
   let me not be put to shame;
   let not my enemies exult over me. (Ps. 25:1–2)

I drank in those words and the assurances that followed, praying them back to God with choking tears. I was comforted to be praying the same words that David had prayed, the same words that Jesus had prayed.

But that wasn't all. Over the next few days, those words came up again and again, in songs and in private conversations. The Holy Spirit personally led me to that truth in my Bible and then spoke it to me again and again through others.

God was satisfying us with his steadfast love.

SATISFIED FOREVER

We were at a church picnic one summer Sunday afternoon before our evening service. Across from us sat an elderly couple we had recently gotten to know through our small group. Between mouthfuls of chili dog, I asked her how they were doing.

She turned her good ear toward me and gave me a puzzled look, so I asked again, more loudly. "Oh," she tipped her head to one side with a quiet smile, "you know. Our days are much the same."

Her husband hunched beside her in his wheelchair, busy with his dinner.

"It's hard. Sometimes I envy those who are free to come and go as they please, to visit their children and play with their grandchildren." Her tired eyes brightened. "But when I open my Bible and read, I become content."

She got up from the table while I pondered her words. There it was. "Satisfy me in the morning with your steadfast love." Her contentment amazed me. Even the change in her countenance was visible evidence of God's steadfast love to her. I could see that God means for us to "rejoice and be glad all our days," even in the wilderness. He really does.

The woman returned with a big smile and an enormous bowl of ice cream for her husband. "I'm sorry, dear, but they were all out of small bowls . . ."

He winked at me. "You see; I can always count on her to take good care of me. That's why I won't send anyone else to get my ice cream."

Comedy or Tragedy?

Is the story of hunger a tragedy or a comedy? If it is a tragedy, it will end with frustration and cynicism, mocking and bitter emptiness. The end will look like Jesus hanging on the cross, surrounded by mockers and cynics, every promise failed, every hope dashed.

But if this story is a comedy, it will turn every disappointment on its head and will leave us laughing in shocked amazement. The end of the story will look like Jesus not just risen from death but eating and drinking and laughing with us all. *Satisfaction* is too weak a word to cover it.

Where will hunger end? That question began our chapter. But now we can conclude, *It will end with satisfaction, because Jesus* "*is the propitiation for our sins, and not for ours only but also for the sins of the whole world*" *(1 John 2:2).*

Because Jesus has inserted himself into our story, our story has been swept up into his. Judging from his earthly life, he seems to have a preference for parties and for sharing them with sinners. When he turned water into wine at the wedding in Cana, it was just a foretaste of the full feast that awaits us.

Here's Isaiah's vision of it:

> On this mountain the LORD of hosts will make for all peoples
> a feast of rich food, a feast of well-aged wine,
> of rich food of marrow, of aged wine well refined.
> And he will swallow up on this mountain
> the covering that is cast over all peoples,
> the veil that is spread over all nations.
> He will swallow up death forever;
> and the Lord GOD will wipe away tears from all faces,
> and the reproach of his people he will take away from all
> the earth,
> for the LORD has spoken. (Isa. 25:6–8)

Hope deferred will be a thing of the past, because "desire fulfilled is a tree of life." The tree of life will be there, its fruit ripe and ready for our taking (Rev. 22:2).

Will Morning Ever Come?

Our grandson fell out of bed the first night he was at our house this summer. Then he had a nightmare. Then I heard the patter of his feet going down the stairs to check the kitchen clock. Finally, at about four, his little face appeared in our doorway. "Will morning ever come?"

I know how he feels. It will, Brendon, it will.

FOR REFLECTION AND DISCUSSION

1. "Doubt rumbles most loudly when our souls feel empty" (pp. 117–18). When your soul is empty, which question do you tend to ask: "Is God really good?" or "Is God mad at me?"
2. "We treat God like a lazy employee who is on probation" (p. 120). Why is God unworthy of this treatment? Why does he have a right to be angry with us?
3. "A satisfied God is my hope for satisfaction" (p. 123). How does the obedience and death of Jesus answer both of the questions in question 1?
4. How do Psalm 90:14 and the story of the manna point to daily satisfaction in this life? Can you remember a time when God's steadfast love became real to you?
5. Does your life feel like a tragedy or a comedy (in the classical sense of having a happy ending) right now? How does the end of Jesus' story give you hope for how your own story will end?

Interlude

Cleansing the Palate

When cooking, invest time. Or work. Not both.
—*Mark Bittman,* New York Times

In the first half of the book, we've learned *why* we need to feed on Jesus. We've tasted bits of his goodness and experienced what it means for him to be our true food. Every one of these morsels is found on the pages of the Bible. Now we need to learn *how* to feed on Jesus in our Bibles.

It's time to learn to cook. It's time for us to learn how to see Jesus for ourselves, whether we're outsiders still investigating the Christian faith or insiders convinced that Jesus is our true food.

What a prospect! If seeing Jesus through someone else's eyes has been compelling, how much more thrilling will it be to see him firsthand as the Holy Spirit opens your eyes to understand the Scriptures? That aha moment brings greater satisfaction than solving a mental or spiritual puzzle.

That moment is nothing less than a face-to-face encounter with the living God through the pages of his living word.

ALL OR NOTHING?

Our initial enthusiasm about this prospect may be enough to get us started, but from the beginning I want to prepare us to keep going. I've started and abandoned projects often enough to be realistic. Here's my caution—don't take the all-or-nothing approach. It's as they say: you'll end up with nothing every time.

We might think that taking the Bible seriously means we have to study it on a heroic level, with charts and commentaries and colored pencils, for at least an hour a day, minimum, because anything less means that we're not committed.

I'll give you a simpler method in part 2. We'll practice our skills by using them to study Paul's letter to Philemon, found in the New Testament. If you have an hour a day to do the practice sessions, that's lovely. But if you have only a half hour, you can still do it. Even if you have only fifteen minutes, that can still be enough.

Most of us have been through periods in our lives when personal time is squeezed almost to nothing. Circumstances such as a move, a new baby, sickness, depression, job changes, deadlines for students (and teachers), and family emergencies cause us to switch to survival mode.

Even after the crisis passes, fifteen minutes still may be all the time you have to spend in God's Word. That can be discouraging, unless you take a long-term perspective.

INVEST

If fifteen minutes is all you have, then don't just spend it. *Invest* it. Don't let it dwindle away to nothing. And don't despise the time just because it's small. Grab it and make use of it. Guard it. It's not just "better than nothing"; it's an investment that will produce dividends over time.

We've all heard that small investments add up to big gains. Well, just fifteen minutes a day spent in Bible study will add up to

- almost two hours a week
- almost eight hours a month
- over ninety hours a year

That's more than two forty-hour workweeks each year spent getting to know the true God through the Scriptures. Amazing.

A PARABLE

We often waste the precious time we have by lamenting that we don't have more. Jesus knew firsthand about limitations, since by the incarnation he took on the limits of time and space. He squeezed himself into a body that needed food and sleep and daily care, one day at a time. He couldn't be in two places at once any more than you and I can.

Jesus also knows the temptations that our limits cause us to experience—to complain about those limits, to compare and make excuses and fritter away the precious resources that we've been given.

So Jesus tells the parable of the talents[1] to help us to know how to live fully within those limits, between now and when he returns. He begins, "It will be like a man going on a journey, who called his servants and entrusted to them his property" (Matt. 25:14).

Each servant is given a different amount to manage, but the task of each is the same. Each is to use his portion, invest it, and cause it to grow until his master returns.

1. "A talent was a monetary unit worth about twenty years' wages for a laborer" (from the footnote to Matthew 25:15 in the *ESV Study Bible* [Wheaton, IL: Crossway, 2008]). We use the term today to refer to any and all resources that God has entrusted to us until Christ returns.

Upon his return, the master doesn't compare the output of the servants. He isn't impressed that the five-talent man made five talents more. He isn't disappointed that the two-talent man made only two more. He is looking for faithfulness.

In fact, he says the exact same words to these two servants, not just commending them but rewarding and celebrating their faithfulness. "Well done, good and faithful servant. You have been faithful over a little; I will set you over much. Enter into the joy of your master" (Matt. 25:21, 23).

Can you imagine being told this about your fifteen minutes when Christ returns?

THE FAITHFUL SERVANT

At this point, my heart sinks again. If this is about my faithfulness, I'm not so reassured. "Good and faithful servant"? Not me. I know that I'll blow it. I won't always be diligent to guard even my fifteen-minute window.

It's true that you and I won't be perfectly faithful in investing our time and talents as we should. But Jesus was. You see, in the parable Jesus plays two parts. He's the Master who leaves and returns, but he's also the Faithful Servant. He faithfully used every limited resource entrusted to him in his earthly life. Perfectly. Then he died and rose again, to give us a perfect investment portfolio to present before the returning Master.

If Jesus can satisfy God's perfect standard of faithfulness, I need to let him satisfy my inner drive for perfection too. Instead of my all-or-nothing approach, he invites me to work hard while resting in his perfect work.

He wants me to enter his joy.

Here's the bottom line. If you have an hour a day, use it. But if you have only fifteen minutes, don't sweat it. Invest it and reap joy.

PART TWO

PLENTY

Seven

Come

*The way to entice people into cooking
is to cook delicious things.
—Yotam Ottolenghi*

*Come, everyone who thirsts, come to the waters;
and he who has no money, come, buy and eat!
—Isaiah 55:1*

"Excuse me. . . . Do you actually do this?"

A young mom approached me after the session. I'd been teaching the material that is coming up in the next three chapters, and she looked troubled.

"I need to know, because I honestly can't imagine doing this in my life right now."

She told me about her three-year-old with autism, a child who rarely napped and who needed her constant attention. On top of that, she had given birth to a second child six months before who still wasn't sleeping through the night.

We sat down together. This was one hungry woman. She needed wisdom on a minute-by-minute basis. She needed creativity, patience, and a sense of humor. She craved adult companionship.

And she definitely needed a nap. The last thing I wanted to do was to add to her burden.

Then I remembered my own struggles as a mom. The ups and downs of sleep wreaked havoc with my moods. My mood swings made me feel alternately angry or depressed. I had floundered in that new stage of life, looking for some solid ground under my feet.

My husband saw it better than I did. He saw my emotional ups and downs, and he saw my struggle to trust God with these new challenges. He knew my faith needed to be fed.

One day he brought it up. "I know that you need lots of help these days, and I want to help you with the baby or the dishes or whatever, but I think there's something else you need."

As soon as he'd said he would help with the dishes, I was all ears.

"You need to know how much God loves you. Let me free you up to spend time with him."

ORDINARY PEOPLE

That's what I told the young mom that day. Not that she needed to get her act together. Not that she needed to add Bible study to her never-ending list of things to do. But that she needed to hear how much God loves her in Christ. Right now. Today. And then again tomorrow.

And, yes, she could definitely use her husband's support, not to mention the help of a friend or two.

I wanted her to see that her need to feed on Jesus was greater than all the other needs she felt. Even more, I wanted her to see God's eagerness to nourish her with Christ. That's why God was calling her to come—not just to the kitchen but to the table.

In the next three chapters, we'll learn to prepare a meal for ourselves from our Bibles. We're not trying to become Bible experts. But neither are we snatching verses out of context and believing them without understanding. We're looking for a sustainable way to feed on Jesus in our Bibles that we can do over the long haul—fifteen minutes at a time, year after year.

Who has time for this? Anyone who's hungry. We've all been through times in our lives when we were too busy to cook, but our hunger drove us to figure out some way to get food into our stomachs. We may have had to change our approach, even to try some unconventional methods, but we didn't go hungry.

While our hunger will provide forceful motivation to find food, I want you to know that it's not simply up to us. We have a God who feeds the hungry. He wants us to sit down with his Word and prepare a meal for ourselves. He also wants us to stay and enjoy it.

He is the host who says, "Come."

Who the Bible Was Written For

The Bible was written for ordinary people like you and me. People working swing shift. People diagnosed with cancer. People who forgot to pay their electric bills. That's why God bothered to write it all down—because he wants us to read and understand and believe.

He wrote it so that we can have faith.

> That is why [Abraham's] faith was "counted to him as righteousness." But the words "it was counted to him" were not written for his sake alone, but for ours also. (Rom. 4:22–24)

We study to understand what true faith is and why it counts as righteousness.

God wrote it so that we can have hope. "For whatever was written in former days was written for our instruction, that through endurance and through the encouragement of the Scriptures we might have hope" (Rom. 15:4).

We study to understand what this hope is and why, unlike our other hopes, it won't let us down.

God wrote it so that we can have love. "In this is love, not that we have loved God but that he loved us and sent his son to be the propitiation for our sins" (1 John 4:10).

We study to see what true love looks like in the life and death of Jesus and why our love is always a response to his.

God knows that we need faith, hope, and love on a regular basis. So he wrote all these words for us. But let's not just *talk* about who the Bible was written for; let's see it firsthand. Come with me to a house in the village of Bethany. Lean on the doorframe and peek in for a minute.

Martha, Martha

It's dark inside. After our eyes adjust, the first thing we notice is the activity in the kitchen. A woman stirs the pot, pounds circles of bread dough, pulls pita from the hearth, tosses it into a basket, and scurries out of the room. She returns moments later with an empty basket, wipes her face, snatches a basket of fruit and dashes out again.

We don't dare interrupt her to ask a question, so we peek into the other room. There we see a completely different scene. A woman sits listening on the floor. A man sits on the only stool, teaching her.

What's happening here? We can read the five verses in a few minutes (Luke 10:38–42). Jesus is a guest in this home, welcomed and served by Martha, while her sister Mary sits and listens. Martha tells Jesus to order Mary to help her, but Jesus knows that Martha doesn't need Mary's help. She needs him.

It takes us only a few minutes to observe the details of what happened and to see the interplay of the characters. Most of us identify with Martha. We hear Jesus' words to Martha as a rebuke to us and feel guilty about being too busy to read our Bibles.

Then we rush off to clean up the kitchen or dash to our morning commute.

But there's more here. We have already observed Jesus as a character in the story, but we haven't yet seen him in his saving work.

Not One Disciple, But Two

Jesus may have been invited as a guest for dinner, but he intends to feed these two women. He wants *both of them* to know him as the Christ, their Messiah, and to become his disciples.

Watch him treat Mary like a disciple. Contrary to the culture of the day, he's instructing her in the Scriptures *as if she were one of the Twelve.* He's opening her mind to understand the Bible, so that she can know that the Scriptures point to him.

Mary must understand his teaching as she hears it. That's the only explanation for the actions she will take a year later. Jesus will be her guest again. The dinner will celebrate the raising of Mary and Martha's brother Lazarus, and Jesus will be the guest of honor.

One year later, Mary won't be sitting at Jesus' feet; she'll be kneeling there, breaking open a fabulously expensive perfume bottle and anointing him. She has kept the perfume for the day of his burial.[1] How has she known to do this? His word has taken root in her. Her actions will be the worship of a true disciple.

Today Jesus is also inviting Martha to sit and eat. He wants to nourish her with the story of his saving love.

I want us to hear his invitation to us too.

THE INVITATION

Don't you love to get an invitation in the mail? You pull the stack of paper out of your mailbox and sort through it before

---

1. John 12:7 (translation in note).

you even go inside—advertisements, catalogues, mass mailings, bills. Then you see it. An invitation addressed to you. Hand lettered. Good paper.

Someone is requesting "the pleasure of your company." You feel special.

Electronic invitations don't quite do it, do they? We usually see them when we're trying to catch up on e-mail. *Oh, bother. One more thing to do.* With one eye on the clock, we open the invitation and check the date. *I guess I could make it, but I'll have to rearrange some things. I wonder who's coming?*

You check the guest list and realize that quite a crowd has been invited. *Maybe they wouldn't miss me.* You look over the replies. The few people who have committed to coming so far aren't really your type. *I don't think I'll commit yet. Maybe in a few days.*

God's Invitation

God's invitation comes to us through the prophet Isaiah: "Come, everyone who thirsts, come to the waters; and he who has no money, come, buy and eat! Come, buy wine and milk without money and without price" (Isa. 55:1).

God is insistent, almost pushy. Come, come, come, *come!* Four times we are invited. He must really mean it. Apparently there's no cover charge either, which is good because it's the end of the month and I'm out of money. It sounds like he's got both the food and drink covered.

Maybe I should offer to bring something?

But this is not a potluck. It's a feast put on by the Lord himself. He has spread his table, and now he invites us to come and eat. This is the free invitation of the gospel, coming right on the heels of a prophecy about the Suffering Servant who will atone for our sin (Isa. 52:13–53:12).

It's gospel. Do you hear the good news in it? God is saying, "Come. This meal is free because I've already paid. It's ready because I've already done all the work. You don't need to bring anything. Just come and eat!"

This is the "come to Jesus" invitation offered freely to all. It's an invitation to believe the gospel, not just for the first time but for every day after. It's an invitation to hear his words and feed our souls. "Listen diligently to me, and eat what is good, and delight yourselves in rich food" (Is. 55:2).

The guest list for this feast is unbelievably long. And you and I are on it.

The Reluctant Guests

But we hesitate. All of us are reluctant guests at one time or another.

Some of us hesitate because the invitation sounds too good to be true. We may be considering the gospel for the first time. Or we may have tried Christianity for a while and become disillusioned. We're convinced that it's a bait-and-switch situation. Sure, it sounds free, but what's it like once you're in? We want to see the fine print, the hidden costs. We're the suspicious.

Some of us hesitate because we're busy. Like Martha, we're preoccupied with all the stuff we have to do for Jesus, including study our Bibles. We're so busy saying yes to the many needs around us that we haven't realized we're saying no to God. We've become addicted to serving, and now it feels wrong to sit down. We're the distracted.

Some of us hesitate because we feel undeserving. We feel like we need to clean ourselves up first, or at least pay for the mess we've made. We don't want him to see us like this. We've binged or crashed or fallen or failed. We hold back so that we can punish ourselves before we come to the table. We're the ashamed.

Some of us aren't hesitating—we're simply overwhelmed. We are the weary, buried under our circumstances, like the woman in the opening story. Drowning in our duties. But by far the biggest burdens that we carry are ourselves. Somehow, we feel, we should be able to handle this. What's wrong with us? Everyone else seems to be doing fine with his or her load. We're the crushed.

The suspicious. The distracted. The ashamed. The crushed. We who hesitate are the very ones who need this good news the most.

Hear the Good News Again

Why do we hesitate? Saying yes to any invitation means saying no to something else. Martha had to leave her serving in order to come. What might God be asking us to leave so that we can come?

Here are some suggestions:

- The suspicious one may need to leave her cynicism.
- The distracted one may need to turn from her doing to the one who did it all for her.
- The ashamed one may need to turn from punishing herself and hiding her scars behind fig leaves.
- The crushed one may need to turn from making her sense of failure into her identity.

Isaiah 55 calls us to turn from our own ways so that we can return to God. Why? Because our thoughts are not God's thoughts. Our ways are not his ways. Cynicism. Saving ourselves. Punishing ourselves. Defining ourselves. These are not God's ways.

But they can become our ways. Turning from them feels hard. Our thoughts have become our mental habits. Our ways have become our comfortable rut.

Turning feels hard, but it's worth it. Whenever we turn to the Lord, whether for the first or the hundredth time, we will find compassion, pardon, and love. Why? Because of the finished work of Jesus Christ for us. He poured out his life for us so that he could pour out his love into us day after day through the Holy Spirit (Rom. 5:1–5).

Every time we return to him, we hear the gospel again. We need to hear this good news every day.

Come to Me

Jesus fleshes out God's invitation from Isaiah 55 for us. He changes it from audio to video. We see him look at Martha's harried face. We hear him respond to Martha's impatient words with his implied invitation, "Martha, Martha, *won't you come, too*?"

Jesus takes the simple word *come* from Isaiah 55 and makes it personal. "Come to me," he invites each of us—the suspicious, the distracted, the ashamed, the crushed. "Come to me, all who labor and are heavy laden, and I will give you rest" (Matt. 11:28). Don't just come—come to *me*.

We've heard the invitation. Now it's time to see our host.

THE HOST

Barbara. She really knew how to roll out the red carpet.

I had just moved to town when I met her. Within minutes she invited me to her book club. I told her that I was still unpacking, but she brushed every excuse away. "You've got to come. It'll be so much fun. You need this!"

I let her talk me into it. Somehow I got the book and left the mess and found her house and walked up to the door wondering what I was doing there.

Before I'd even rung the bell, she flung open the door. "You came!" She had the biggest smile I'd ever seen. "I'm so excited! I hoped you would!" She was practically jumping up and down like a six-year-old.

You would think I was her long-lost friend, but I was a stranger she'd scooped up off the street and welcomed into her life. I didn't have much choice. She was a host who was determined to welcome me, no matter how much I dragged my heels.

A persistent host is the answer to a reluctant guest.

The Persistent Host

Martha may have invited Jesus into her house, but Jesus turned the tables on her when he invited her to sit at his feet. Did she ever sit down that day? We aren't told.

But he persisted. John 11:1–27 records another day when Jesus came to her. Like the first time, she had invited him, except this time her invitation was a call for help. Her brother Lazarus was very sick. She knew how much Jesus loved Lazarus, and she expected him to drop everything and come. But he didn't. By the time he got there, it was too late. Lazarus had been dead for four days.

Martha came to meet Jesus, not with open arms but with her own plan to fix his mistake. "If you had been here. . . . But even now I know that whatever you ask from God . . ." (vv. 21–22). Martha was busy again, holding back her disappointment, making excuses for his tardiness, offering him a second chance. *OK, you blew it, but at least ask God to do something. It's not too late for the Almighty!*

Her half-formed faith sounds like so many prayers I've said or heard others say: "I hope you can help, Lord. But if you don't, it's okay. I'll figure something out to get you off the hook. You're probably just busy helping all those other people."

Jesus didn't take Martha's advice. He hadn't come to meet her expectations but to blow them up. He was inviting her to his feast again—and he would be her host.

He offered an appetizer. "Your brother will rise again" (v. 23).

She politely refused, "I know . . . in the resurrection on the last day" (v. 24).

Then he pulled out the main course. "I am the resurrection and the life" (v. 25).

Jesus knew the food that Martha needed that day. She didn't need her small plate to be filled by the healing of her brother. She needed her hands to be empty so that he could hand her the heavy platter dripping with his divine power over life and death. She didn't need more of the Jesus whom she thought she knew. She needed a bigger Jesus.

Jesus was a very persistent host that day. He had planned this particular meal ever since he had gotten the call to come. The crowd was assembled; the tomb was opened. When he called Lazarus from the tomb, everyone standing there saw the sign. But *only Martha* got to hear the inside story of what the sign was pointing to.

Jesus didn't love just Lazarus; he also loved Martha. He welcomed her to a table set for one.

The Host Who Serves Us

Martha was so busy serving Jesus that she didn't realize he wanted to serve her. We're the same way. Our confusion is understandable. After all, he is the Lord. We assume that we're taking our proper place when we do the serving.

That's our proper place when we're serving the tables of the people around us. But first we're invited to sit at God's table.

At his table Jesus serves us, just as he served the Twelve. After he washed their feet, he sat down. "Take, eat; this is my body" (Matt. 26:26). He provides the food and passes it to each of us—the bread, his perfect life; the wine, his atoning death. He serves us his life not just in the Supper, which we eat at church, but in the Scriptures, which we hear at church and read at home.

But, we may protest, how can we sit down and eat when we are so busy and burdened? That's the point. We have to leave our sacrifice in order to feed on his.

The antidote for our cynicism and our busyness and our shame and our weariness is to hear the good news again. Jesus finished his work. Now we're free to do our work.

Why is our host so persistent about serving us? He knows our tendency to turn his good news into bad news. For example:

- *Jesus paid for all my sins.* How am I doing at paying him back?
- *I am saved by faith, not works.* How's my faith today—strong enough?
- *God gave his one and only Son for me.* So what am I going to do for him today?

Jesus invites us, by the illuminating power of his Spirit, to read and believe the greatest good news that turns every piece of bad news in this sad, fallen world on its head. It's the news flash of what God has done for us, not what we need to do for him: "that Christ died for our sins in accordance with the Scriptures . . . that he was buried . . . that he was raised on the third day . . . and that he appeared" (1 Cor. 15:3–5).

That's the meal our host wants to serve us today.

The Host Who Sits with Us

Jesus doesn't just serve us. He also sits and eats with us. It's a breakfast date. Or a lunch date. Or a dinner date. Or a middle of the night date. Just with him.

The purpose of the covenant is relationship, remember? That's why God initiated it in the first place. And that's why Jesus came to fulfill it for us. Now we can sit and eat together the way people do when they are friends. Because, now that he's finished his work, that's what we are. Friends.

"Behold, I stand at the door and knock" (Rev. 3:20). We tend to think that this is an invitation for the outsider to believe in Jesus for the first time. "He's knocking on the door of your heart," we say. "Open the door and invite him in!"

However, these words were written to a church. They are the words of a master coming home after a long journey.[2] Traditionally, such a master would expect his servants to jump up and let him in so that he could sit down and eat while they waited on him.[3] This was the way it usually went. The servants stood while the master dined.

That's why these words are surprising. Jesus invited his original hearers to open the door. They had become complacent and weren't listening for his knock. This was a wake-up call for them. But if they opened the door, he wouldn't blast them or make them serve him; he would sit down and eat with them. "If anyone hears my voice and opens the door, I will come in to him and eat with him, and he with me" (Rev. 3:20).

This invitation is for us, too. The Master has become our host, not just serving us but sitting with us. This is his standing invitation.

He invites us to prepare our meal from the Scriptures and then to sit down and eat it—with him.

THE TABLE

So we take him up on his invitation. We sit down to study a Bible passage with high hopes for the meal ahead. But at the end of our allotted time, we look around at what we've prepared. It's pretty scanty. We have some scattered observations. A reasonable effort at placing this page of our Bibles into the big story. And several attempts at seeing Jesus.

Not much of a meal.

2. Taken from study note on Rev. 3:19–20 in the *ESV Study Bible* (Wheaton IL: Crossway, 2008).

3. Jesus makes this normal expectation clear in Luke 17:7–10.

Actually, we think it's pathetic. We were hoping for something better, but we've produced nothing more than peanut butter and jelly. How can this be enough? We came to the table with so many needs—insatiable longings, cyclical sin struggles, intractable family problems, endless money shortages. We ask ourselves, *How can my feeble efforts satisfy my gnawing hungers?*

Because he makes it enough. He makes it plenty.

Lucky Accidents, Great Discoveries, and the Prepared Mind

We bring our sack lunch to God's table, and he multiplies it.

We're like the little boy with the five loaves and two fish (John 6:1–12). We're children, all of us. Our contribution is so small, yet the Lord takes it and delights to use it. That's the astonishing thing about his miraculous feeding of five thousand families with a little boy's lunch. Not that he was able to multiply it, but that he used it at all.

Jesus was perfectly able to make bread from nothing. He had created something out of nothing in the beginning. He could have said, "Let there be lunch!" and it would have been so. But he didn't. He chose to take the child's lunch that he had received from the hands of those bigger children, his disciples, and make it enough.

In the same way, he chooses to use our work of studying the Scriptures and blesses it so that it is enough.

Our preparation readies us to receive what he will give us. Some detail that didn't seem relevant when we first observed it becomes shockingly applicable. The effort to find Jesus suddenly gives us insight. The verse that we memorized last year provides a missing link. The Holy Spirit uses our preparation.

It reminds me of a lecture I heard forty-five years ago, "Lucky Accidents, Great Discoveries, and the Prepared Mind."[4]

4. Hubert Alyea (1903–96), professor emeritus at Princeton University, was known for

An eccentric chemistry professor raced back and forth across the podium, setting off explosions, shooting water pistols, and spraying the audience with carbon dioxide. The entire time he talked about science.

"Why do research? Why even bother? Why all those hours in the laboratory, working on experiments that seem to have nothing to do with real life? How is it relevant? What possible good will it do?"

Then he told us about Isaac Newton. "That apple was a lucky accident. You can be sure that many apples had fallen on many heads in the history of the world before that time. Why did that apple lead him to the discovery of the law of gravity? Because Isaac Newton had a prepared mind."

In the same way, our regular times in the Bible, accumulated over weeks and years, prepare us for the moment when the Holy Spirit drops an apple on our heads.

Suddenly, it's not just enough. It's a gracious plenty.

Plenty

Jesus makes it plenty because he loves us. The one who created us also sustains us, not on the scarcity of our efforts alone, but on the plenty of his love.

He sees the young mom with the three-year-old with autism and the nursing six-month-old. He knows that she doesn't have even fifteen minutes to spend in his Word. Not during the day anyway. But her limitations don't limit him.

God nourishes her with his Word and Spirit in any way she is able to receive them. Through songs in the night. Through

---

this lecture, which he gave on hundreds of occasions. Portions of it are available online under "'Lucky Accidents, Great Discoveries, and the Prepared Mind,' by Hubert N. Alyea, circa 1985," YouTube video, 28:26, from Princeton University Archives audiovisual collection (AC047), posted by "Princeton Campus Life," July 22, 2010, https://www.youtube.com/watch?v=jSw7cHfxbu8.

verses memorized years before. Through the preached Word. Through five minutes snatched here and there, sometimes when she's hiding in the bathroom.

He feeds her because he loves her. He invites her to come.

"Come" is God's invitation to each of us—singles, wives, young moms, single moms, career women. He invites us to come, sit at his table, and fill up on his never-failing love for us in Christ Jesus.

Jesus fulfilled all the conditions of the covenant so that we could sit down and eat with him. He wants to change us from slaves into daughters. He wants to reassure us that he loves us apart from what we produce or fail to produce. He is eager to sustain our lives with his.

So come. In the next chapter, we'll begin to prepare the meal.

FOR REFLECTION AND DISCUSSION

1. "The Bible was written for ordinary people like you and me" (p. 139). Do you agree with that statement? Why or why not?
2. "We have already observed Jesus as a character in the story, but we haven't yet seen him in his saving work" (p. 141). What does that mean? Is the story of Mary and Martha about their performance or about his invitation? Explain.
3. Which of the reluctant guests do you identify with—the suspicious, the distracted, the ashamed, the crushed? Take a moment to put your own reluctance into words.
4. Jesus is the persistent host who overcomes our reluctance. Which example of his persistence convinces you (with Martha, at the Lord's Supper, or as the knocking master)? Why is he so eager to have us sit and eat?
5. God uses our work of studying the Scriptures and blesses it so that it is enough. How does John 6:1–13, the story of the feeding of the five thousand, encourage your small efforts at Bible study?

Eight

Prep

*Technique must be acquired, and, with technique, a
love of the very processes of cooking. . . . If a cook is
willing simply to look at what he is doing, there is hope.*
—Robert Farrar Capon

The moment of truth had arrived. "What should we have for dinner?" I asked my newlywed husband. "Chicken?" he suggested helpfully. I pulled a whole chicken out of the freezer and stared at it in all its frozen, naked, headless glory.

I had learned lots of important things during my childhood, but how to cook a chicken was not one of them.

My mother didn't love to cook. There were several reasons for this. For one thing, Dad delivered babies, so his presence at the dinner table was hit or miss. It's disheartening to any cook when the only person who might actually appreciate her meal either delays it until it becomes an overcooked mess or else bolts out the door as soon as she serves it.

The other places at Mom's dinner table were occupied by us three children. Like most kids, we were picky—picky eaters who liked to pick fights with each other. Mom did her best, putting food on the table and trying to steer the dinner conversation into some sort of demilitarized zone. I think the whole thing disheartened her. She removed her many creative talents from the kitchen and took them elsewhere.

Consequently, I entered my marriage with only two recipes under my belt: cinnamon toast (from Betty Crocker's Cookbook for Boys and Girls) and Toll House cookies (from the back of the package). Cinnamon toast was made in three steps. The Toll House cookies were more involved but worth the effort.

So here I was, staring down a frozen bird that lost the contest only because it couldn't stare back.

The moment of truth had arrived. We were hungry, and we could no longer afford takeout or presume on dinner invitations. I had to learn to cook.

GETTING STARTED

We've come to the same moment in our book. God may have sent the manna, but his people had to gather it and then boil, bake, or fry it into breakfast. In the same way, we need to learn to prepare a simple meal for ourselves from our Bibles.

The rest of this book lays out a method for doing that. It's one thing to be fed by others. Many of us take in biblical teaching through sermons,[1] podcasts, books, articles, and blogs. Those sources are valuable. But learning to feed ourselves is a vital step in growing up.

It can also be daunting.

Overwhelmed by the Options

When we first start learning to cook, it's easy to be overwhelmed by the number of cookbooks out there. We can be

---

1. I'll talk about the central role of the preached gospel in your own local church in chapter 12.

buried by the assumptions they make, too. "Take a heavy enameled stock pot . . ." What if I don't have one of those? Do I need to go out and buy one before I can move on to the next step? Or how about this one: "Take one large mango, seeded and diced. . . ." Sounds yummy, but how do I get the big seed out of the mango without turning the rest of it into pulp?

I've been there. I know how it feels to be a beginner cook, overwhelmed by the mountain of knowledge I don't have.

I was once equally clueless about studying my Bible. All I knew was a jumble of Bible stories from my childhood and a single verse that had caught my attention as a teenager. It had jumped off the page at me during a small group I had started attending: "For I do not understand my own actions. For I do not do what I want, but I do the very thing I hate" (Rom. 7:15).

I couldn't believe it. It felt like someone had been reading my mind. I was awakened to the thought that the Bible was more than a book of children's stories. God wanted to speak to me right now. I wanted more. I wanted to hear his voice and understand what he was saying to me. I wanted to know what was in that book.

But where to start? The options, once again, were overwhelming.

The Hungry Teenager

Let's go back to the hungry teenager we met in the introduction. He's standing in front of the open refrigerator, gaping at its random contents. He knows that he's hungry, but he doesn't yet see the makings of a meal. How can we help him?

If I were to simplify cooking to the basics, I'd tell him that there are only three steps. Prep. Cook. Eat.

Prep involves taking things apart. We get ready to cook by getting out our ingredients and tools (more about these later). Then we start chopping, measuring, slicing, pouring, mincing, and grating. Once we have finished, there are little piles of ingredients all over the counter, but they're not a meal yet.

Cook involves putting things back together. If our ingredients can be eaten raw, we're all set. But if they can't, we'll need to apply heat. We make a meal by assembling what we've prepped and cooking it, if necessary.

Eat involves, well, eating. No one needs to teach a teenager that. But it's helpful to see that the goal of cooking isn't a finished task but a finished meal. A full stomach.

The consensus on Bible study methods gives a very similar picture. At its most basic, Bible study involves three steps: observation, interpretation, and application. *Observation* involves paying careful attention to what's there—taking it apart, in a sense. *Interpretation* involves understanding what it means—putting it back together so that you see the whole picture. And *application*? Well, that's the eating, the payoff of a satisfied soul.

Here's how they line up:

Prep	Observe
Cook	Interpret
Eat	Apply

8.1 The Three Steps of Bible Study

This chapter is about step one: prepping our meal. But before we prep our ingredients, we need to prep ourselves.

PREPPING THE COOK

When we're hungry, we get impatient. We want food *now*. The thought of going into the kitchen and preparing a meal sounds like a lot of work and, frankly, feels discouraging. That's why we so often reach for convenience foods or pick up something already prepared on our way home.

The same thing happens when our souls are hungry. We feel a need. It makes us weak or sad or anxious or confused or frustrated. We want help now. The thought of opening our Bibles and trying to make a meal from scratch sounds like too much work. Frankly, it sounds impossible.

So we open our Bibles to a familiar verse that has comforted us in the past. Or we open at random, looking for some inspiration or guidance. Or we don't open our Bibles at all but instead read what someone else has prepared from its pages.

Those shortcuts can help us to survive in an emergency, but God has something better for our long-term health. He intends his Word to nourish us so that we thrive, not just survive.

Silenced by Sadness

Our need reminds me of the two disciples who were walking the seven-mile road from Jerusalem to Emmaus (Luke 24:13–35). They barely noticed the road, because their thoughts were focused on what had just happened. Only three days before, the very man they had put all their hopes in—Jesus of Nazareth—had been arrested, tried, and executed by crucifixion. He was dead.

They couldn't believe it. Their hopes had been blown apart, and now they were picking through the debris, shocked, sad, hungry to make sense of it all.

Just then a stranger caught up with them and joined them. "What are you talking about?" They stopped, silenced by sadness. Finally, one of them answered, spilling out the story about Jesus, his miracles and teaching, his betrayal and death. To top it off, today they had heard wild rumors flying around that Jesus was alive again. They didn't know what to think.

That's when the stranger spoke. "You shouldn't be surprised by this. The prophets told us that this had to happen to the Christ, that he had to suffer first. But that's not the end of the story." Then he went on to explain the big picture. "And beginning with Moses and all the Prophets, he interpreted to them in all the Scriptures the things concerning himself" (v. 27).

Concerning *himself.* The very one whom the two disciples were grieving was standing right in front of them! It was Jesus who was talking with them. We readers already know it, but they didn't. Their eyes wouldn't be opened to his identity until several hours later, but even now their hearts burned within them as he began to explain the Scriptures.

This reminds me of our dilemma. We're standing here feeling empty and abandoned, while the risen Jesus stands right in front of us, on the pages of our Bibles.

He wants to open our eyes to see him there.

That Very Day . . . and Every Day After

"That very day . . ." That's how the Emmaus road incident begins. What day was it? The very day Jesus rose from the dead. This wasn't just the day of the empty tomb. This was the day that everything changed.

Have you ever wished that you could have been with the disciples that day, walking and talking with Jesus, hearing him explain the Scriptures, having your heart leap from heaviness to joy?

You can have something even better than that. When Jesus was with the two disciples, he could only walk *beside* them to teach them. But after he rose from death and ascended to heaven, he sent his Spirit to live *inside* each person who believes. The Holy Spirit, sometimes called the Spirit of Christ,[2] is even closer to believers today than Jesus was to his disciples.

The Holy Spirit was sent to open our eyes to understand the Scriptures.[3] If you're hungry to see Jesus, ask the Holy Spirit for help.

---

2. He is so described in Acts 16:7, Romans 8:9, Galatians 4:6, Philippians 1:19, and 1 Peter 1:11.

3. "These things God has revealed to us through the Spirit. For the Spirit searches

He may have already been at work as you've read this book. Did your heart ever stir with hope when you got to the parts about Jesus in each chapter? That's because the story of our hunger is just one part of the story of the Bible, and the story of the Bible is all about Christ. The Spirit of Jesus helps us to see that.

We won't be prepping this meal alone.

PREPPING THE INGREDIENTS

Before we prep the ingredients, we have to pick what to eat. For the purpose of this book, we'll be practicing our skills on the lovely little New Testament book of Philemon. It's only one chapter long—just twenty-five verses, to be precise. But, as much as I like short books, I'm not picking it just for that reason.

To thrive, we need to understand the Bible. It is meant to be chewed, digested, and absorbed. It's meant to form us into people who can make our toughest decisions. It's meant to motivate us by changing our deepest desires. It's meant to comfort us with solid hope that metabolizes slowly and keeps us steady in a crisis.

To understand the Bible, we have to study it as it was written—in connected paragraphs, not isolated sentences; in books, not verses.[4]

That's why I'm picking Philemon. It tells a story that we can understand together as we learn this method.

Now that we've picked our book, we're ready to assemble our ingredients and tools.

---

everything, even the depths of God" (1 Cor. 2:10).

4. As it is often noted, both the chapter divisions and the verses were added to the Bible in the Middle Ages, in the years 1205 and 1551, respectively. They make it easier to refer to parts of the text, but they weren't part of the original text.

The Ingredients

Now that we have our Bibles open, what ingredients do we pull out and put on the counter? There are four elements present in some form on every page of our Bibles: God, people, the relationship between them, and what happens. You could call them the four basic food groups.

Prep: The Four ingredients	Prep: The Four Tools
God	
People	
The relationship between them	
What happens	

8.2 Bible Study Ingredients

Let's talk for a minute about each one and why it's important.

God

The Bible is first of all a book about God, from the first sentence ("In the beginning, God created the heavens and the earth" [Gen. 1:1]) to the last ("The grace of the Lord Jesus be with all. Amen" [Rev. 22:21]). God is the one who started it all. He is the Creator and also the Author. He is the Author and also the main character.

This may seem obvious, but we need to say it out loud. *The Bible is not first about you and me; it's about God.* If we understand that, it changes two things.

First, it changes *how* we read the Bible. We don't start by looking for ourselves behind every sentence and situation. Instead we start by looking for God. Where does he show up in this passage? What's he up to? We get to know God by spying on him. We eavesdrop on his conversations and watch his actions to understand his character.

Second, knowing that the Bible is first about God changes

why we read the Bible. We open our Bibles not to learn ancient history or to increase our store of Bible trivia but to know a person—his character, the things he commands, the promises he makes, the mercy he shows. We need to know God so that we can trust him. We need to know him *better* so that we can trust him *more*.

Here's a short list of things that you can start looking for. I'll go into more detail in chapter 9.

God's
Character
Commands
Promises
Mercy

8.3 Observing God

People

That said, the Bible is about people as well as God. That isn't my idea; it's God's. He brought people into the story in the very first chapter. People are still around in the very last chapter. In fact, what started as a story about two people ends as a story involving uncounted multitudes from every corner of history and geography. God is so serious about us and our part in the story that he ends his book with an invitation, "Come" (Rev. 22:17), so that more will join the story before it ends.

This too changes how we read the Bible. We read it to understand the people in the story, much as we would read any good biography. We lose ourselves in someone else's story. That in itself is a nice break from our incessant preoccupation with ourselves.

We become curious. What kind of people made it onto the pages of this book? We're surprised to find a vast range: from quite virtuous to terribly evil. There are heroes, villains, sinners, and sufferers. Some characters astound us by their wise words or courageous actions. Others make us shake our heads with disgust. Why don't they ever learn?

Suddenly we catch a glimpse of ourselves in one of them. *Her anxiety sounds like a line from my journal. His self-centered question could have come out of my mouth.* Their lives become a mirror to our own. Despite the cultural difference and historical distance, they sound like relatives. We sit up and pay attention.

Here is a short cast of characters you'll want to keep an eye out for. I'll add detail in chapter 9.

Man or Woman as
Hero
Villain
Sinner
Sufferer

8.4 Observing People

The Relationship between God and People

The third ingredient we pull out of our open Bibles is the relationship between God and the people in this section of the story. God created us for that relationship, but ever since the incident in the garden of Eden, well, it's gotten complicated.

A relationship can be visualized as the space between two people—in this case, between God and a person in the story. Picture person one and person two, then take a look at the space between them. Are they far apart or close together? Are they facing each other, or have one or both turned away? Are they on speaking terms? What are they saying to each other? How are they acting toward each other?

Keep an eye peeled for things that surprise you. People can act in surprising ways, but God's actions hold the biggest surprises.

He says that he'll judge and then he doesn't, or he stops before he's finished.[5]

Don't let things like that sneak by you. Ask why. God isn't like us, changing his mind because he's forgetful or tired or loses his nerve. If he cuts a consequence short, he has a reason. Noticing his surprising behavior sets us up for the next step: understanding the reason behind it. We'll talk about that later.

What Happens

The fourth ingredient is the action of the story. What actually happens in this scene? It could be action packed or relatively quiet. Sometimes the action is in the background of the passage—the event that prompted the psalm or the problem that led to a letter's being written. Sometimes there's no action.

This is probably the easiest question to answer. Even though I've listed it as the fourth ingredient, we'll use it as our first question. Writing down what actually happens in the scene is the quickest way to jump out of our lives and into the passage.

This question also helps us to connect this section of the Bible with the one right before it. "Previously on *Lost* . . ." is the recap line of a TV show that held our attention for seven years. That's a good way to start your answer to the "what happens" question.

When you answer it, be as brief as possible. Just state the facts. Imagine you're writing the lead sentence of a newspaper article or taking notes at a crime scene after the police officer asks, "What seems to be the problem, ma'am?"

God. People. The relationship between them. What happens.

Looking for these four basic food groups in our Bibles will help us to find food there.

Now let's assemble our tools.

5. For example, see the incident from David's life found in 2 Samuel 24:1–17.

TOOLS

Some Bible studies use highlighters, colored pencils, workbooks, and maps. I love these studies. They're especially good if you have structure and accountability. I'm usually excited when they begin and glad when they finally end.

I'm proposing a different kind of study—one that you can do day in and day out, through job changes and babies and moving and menopause. For this kind you'll need a Bible,[6] a pen, and a notebook or journal of some kind.

You'll also need some intangible tools.

Prep: The Four Tangible Tools	Prep: The Four Intangible Tools
Bible	Hunger
Pen	Curiosity
Notebook or journal	Imagination
Study Bible for background	Questions

8.5 Bible Study Tools

Three Creative Tools

Hunger is our first tool. Our hunger drives us to find food. We automatically bring it with us. If we try to ignore it, it will jump up and down like a pop-up ad.

Let's recognize our hunger and consciously bring it to the table. What are we hungry for? We don't always know. So we might journal it—briefly—to God:

Father, I feel like I want to hide this morning. I guess it's shame, but I'm not sure. Maybe it came from that phone call I got from my friend. Can you please help me to label it? And will you please speak to me about it?

6. I like to use the *ESV Study Bible* (Wheaton, IL: Crossway, 2008) to get background information as I start a new book. But while I'm studying I prefer to use a Bible (or app) with cross-references but without commentary.

At that point I can set my hunger aside temporarily and go on with my study. I'm counting on God to speak to my need, but he will have other things to say to me too. I want to be ready to hear them.

Curiosity is an invaluable tool. It's what keeps us reading that page-turner long past the time we should have turned out our lights. The plot drives us, and a skillful writer will make sure to leave us hanging at the end of each chapter so that we immediately start reading the next one.

Few of us read our Bibles that way. We're either too distant from the historical context of the story or too familiar with it. So curiosity is something we have to cultivate. The questions I'll give you will get you started on your study. Answer them, but also let them stimulate questions of your own. "Why?" "What does this mean?"

Imagination is an underused tool in most of our Bible studies. It's what makes a movie come to life as we watch it. The combined talents of actors, directors, costume designers, composers, and editors hook us. We walk into the theater cold, but within fifteen minutes we not only know the characters but care about what happens to them.

When we use our imagination in Bible study, we engage our five senses to bring the story to life. We try to see the scene: Paul in prison. We imagine the smells of his cell, the sound of the chains as he stands. We try to put ourselves in his shoes, to feel a little of what he felt. It changes how we read his words.

Hunger, curiosity, and imagination help us to invest ourselves personally in the open Bible in front of us.

One Precision Tool

Questions. Our last and most important tool is questions. Good questions are like knives. They separate word from word.

They force us to pay attention. They help us to see more than we saw at first. Questions direct our study, focusing it so we don't wander aimlessly around.

I'll bet you've had an experience in which a simple question brought sharp clarity to your life. You're drifting around the mall, waiting to pick up your daughter from soccer practice, when you suddenly remember you were invited to a wedding this weekend.

In a moment you're on a quest, directed by the single burning question: "Where can I find a great but affordable gift for the couple?"

Questions are like that. A good question can change your Bible study from an aimless stroll to a purposeful walk. The secret to effective Bible study is learning to ask the right questions of the passage. But what is the right kind?

The kind that helps us to see the ingredients better.

Seeing the Onion

If you've done even the smallest amount of cooking, you've likely chopped an onion. Wiped your eyes. Then proceeded with the recipe. You and I have seen a lot of onions in our time. But have we ever really *looked at* one?

That's the question the late food critic and Episcopal priest Robert Farrar Capon asks in his book *Supper of the Lamb*. He tells us to pull out our cutting boards to chop the onions for our recipe. Then he challenges us to slow down and use the sharpness of the knife to *see* the onions.

> As nearly as possible now, try to look at it as if you had never seen an onion before. Try, in other words, to meet it on its own terms, not to dictate yours to it. You are convinced, of course, that you know what an onion is. You think perhaps that it is a brownish yellow vegetable, basically spherical in

shape, composed of fundamentally similar layers. All such prejudices should be abandoned.[7]

The biggest obstacle to really seeing the onion (it turns out to be more delicate and beautiful than we realized) is our assumption that we already know what's there. That's the biggest obstacle to really seeing the pages of our Bible, too. We think we already know what's there.

The right questions help us to see what's actually on the page. That's why the right questions can't be just about us—our personal concerns—but need to be about the four ingredients of the passage in front of us: God, the people, the relationship between them, and what happens.

> However, if we start with our questions and only then look to the Bible for answers, we *assume* that we are asking all the right questions—that we properly understand our need. . . . We need not only the Bible's prescription to our problems but also its diagnosis of them.[8]

The right questions help us to see God and, eventually, to see ourselves.

PRACTICE

Now let's put it all together and practice. Here's the plan. Look up the New Testament book of Philemon in your own Bible, or use an online resource.[9]

7. Robert Farrar Capon, *The Supper of the Lamb: A Culinary Reflection* (Garden City, NY: Doubleday, 1969; repr. New York: Modern Library, 2002), 11.

8. Timothy Keller, *Preaching: Communicating Faith in an Age of Skepticism* (New York: Viking, 2015), 97, emphasis added.

9. For example, Philemon in the ESV on Bible Gateway: https://www.biblegateway.com /passage/?version=ESV&search=Philemon%201.

We'll start with *background information* on the book of Philemon. That's where I recommend you start with any new book. A study Bible will provide you with that material in the future, but this time I'll do the work for you.

Then I'll give you the *questions* you'll use to prep the passage.[10]

Finally, we'll do the "fifteen-minute experiment." The goal is not to complete all the questions but to see how far you get in fifteen minutes. The next day, pick up where you left off and invest another fifteen minutes. And the next.

I hope you discover two things. First, even fifteen minutes of prep work can give us something to feed on. We don't have to finish making dinner before we snack on some of the shredded cheese. Second, even a few days of practice begins to increase our skills. This will get easier.

One of my favorite scenes in the movie *Julie & Julia* is when Julia Child begins to attend the elite cooking school Le Cordon Bleu in Paris. The first day, she and the other students are asked to chop onions. The camera pans across the table, showing knives flying in rhythmic precision, then pauses over Julia's cutting board. She chops like a housewife, halting and careful and amateur. The instructor shakes his head and shows her a more professional technique.

The next scene cuts to Julia's kitchen table, a mountain of yellow onions on her left, a mountain of slices on the right. She's practicing her new technique. The tempo of her knife is getting faster.

Background

We're reading the apostle Paul's mail—specifically a personal letter he wrote to a man named Philemon who lived in the city of Colossae in Asia Minor. Paul knew Philemon personally. A

---

10. The questions on the next page are also reproduced in Appendix A as a worksheet.

few years earlier, Philemon had heard the gospel through Paul's preaching and had believed.

Why did Paul write this letter? Philemon was a wealthy slave owner. One of his slaves, named Onesimus, had run away to Rome, possibly stealing money for his journey as well. While in Rome, he had met Paul and become a Christian. For a while Paul discipled him, and Onesimus helped Paul with various needs.

Now Paul was sending Onesimus back to his master, Philemon, along with a letter. He asked Philemon to respond to his runaway slave as a follower of Jesus Christ, not as a typical first-century slaveholder in the Roman Empire.

Prep Questions

1. *What happens here?* Read the entire letter and write a one-to-two-sentence summary that gives the simple facts of the story. (You might use the questions *who, what, when, where,* and *how,* but avoid the question *why.*)

2. *What does it tell me about God?* Focus on the body of the letter—verses 8–20. Observe every mention of God and note what you learn about him: his character, his words, his actions. (If these stir any personal questions you want to ask God, write those in the margin.)

3. *What does it tell me about the people?* Focus on the body of the letter—verses 8–20. Observe Paul first. What do you learn about him? Can you picture him? Then do the same with Philemon and Onesimus. Is anyone a hero, villain, sinner, or sufferer? (If you identify with one person more than the others, make a note in the margin.)

4. *What's the relationship between God and Paul? Between God and Philemon? Between God and Onesimus?* (If anything surprises you about how God relates to each one, put a question mark in the margin.)

The Fifteen-Minute Experiment

When I teach this method in a group setting, we read the passage out loud together, and then I turn off my microphone. After fifteen minutes, I turn it back on and invite the others in the group to share what they've observed.

I'm always amazed at how carefully they've observed what's there. That's the beauty of using questions to help us to focus. I'm also amazed to hear someone observe something that I've missed, even though I've studied this passage numerous times. That's the beauty of group study.

But I'm most amazed at the insights that come from the simple discipline of observation. We haven't yet interpreted the letter, but we are already finding food there.

I hope you do too.

FOR REFLECTION AND DISCUSSION

1. Use the four prep questions to do the fifteen-minute experiment at least once.
2. What was the easiest question for you to answer? The hardest?
3. What surprised you about God?
4. Which character did you identify with? Why?
5. Did anything feed your soul?

Nine

Cook

Take away this pudding; it has no theme.
—attributed to Winston Churchill

Something is revealed in a final scene of Jesus' life that
makes us want to go back to the very beginning of God's
story, and read it again in light of what we know now.
—Nancy Guthrie, The Promised One

My mother could see the castle long before the limousine rolled through the gates and up to the main entrance. She and my sister had traveled thousands of miles for this moment. They were coming to call at Downton Abbey.

The driver opened the door, and she stepped out onto the gravel drive. Leaning on her stylish cane, she looked around at the grounds, the path, the front door. Then she nodded. Satisfactory.

Moments later the door opened, and she was warmly greeted by the hostess, who acted as her guide. They entered Lord Grantham's study. My mother interrupted the docent's speech, lifting her cane and pointing it toward the massive desk that stood in the center of the room.

"That desk"—she gestured with her cane—"is supposed to be there, by the window."

Her guide smiled. "You're very observant. We move it beside the window before filming starts. But at other times we put it back here in the center, where it normally sits."

My mother tilted her head, furnishing her imagination with this new piece of information. She had lived in the story of Downton Abbey ever since the first season of the show. As the DVDs were released, she bought them so that she could play them over and over, picking up more details, delighting in her favorite lines.

She continued her tour, checking each room against the images in her mind. Upstairs in one of the bedrooms, she stopped again and turned to her guide.

"Do you remember when Bates was handcuffed and taken away? What happened to his cane?"

The docent paused, then shook her head. "That's a good question. I don't know."

My mother beamed. Very satisfactory.

LIVING IN ANOTHER STORY

Most of us have spent time living in another story. We take our popcorn into the movie theater hoping that we can lose ourselves for a few hours in someone else's adventure or romance or drama. Unless the movie's really awful, it works. If it's really good, the spell may last for days before it's broken.

For a moment, that story becomes more vivid than our own. Instead of helping us to escape our lives, it helps us to live them. We ponder the words that gave the hero the courage to embark on his quest. They stir our hope. We replay the moment when the child was found, against all odds, and reunited with her parents. It leaves us with longing for more.

Sometimes a story makes such an impression on us that we choose to live in it. We buy the soundtrack so that we can return to it again and again, like my mother did with Downton Abbey. We talk about it with other people who love the show, quoting bits of dialogue to each other, and then laughing at what nerds we are. Sometimes we even dress up as one of the characters and go to the midnight opening of the sequel.

Not that I've ever done that.

The Story of Stories

There is one story that we're all meant to live in. The whole story of the Bible is meant to be the context of our own life stories. Our stories begin to make sense when we place them in that bigger one.

We saw that in part 1 of this book. As we placed the story of our hunger into the whole story of the Bible, it helped us to understand our everyday experiences. It treated our problem of hunger as real. It didn't offer simplistic solutions. It answered some of our questions. It raised questions that we hadn't thought to ask.

And it gave us hope that our hunger can be satisfied.

There's a reason for this. The Bible isn't just a story like all the others. It's the true story behind them all. Why do we return to our favorite stories again and again? We return because we find in them drama so riveting and heroes so compelling and resolutions so satisfying that we wish they would never end. We wish that they were true. And we wish that we could be part of the story.

The Bible is just that. It's the true story with the bravest hero and the most stunning reversal of all.

J. R. R. Tolkien explains why this story feels so satisfying. "Far more important is the Consolation of the Happy Ending," he writes, describing what he calls "the sudden joyous 'turn.'" He goes on: "This joy . . . is a sudden and miraculous grace:

never to be counted on to recur. It does not deny the existence of . . . sorrow and failure: . . . it denies . . . universal final defeat and in so far is *evangelium*, giving a fleeting glimpse of Joy, Joy beyond the walls of the world, poignant as grief."[1]

We know what he means. Just when the movie is darkest, when every means of escape has been cut off and the enemy is closing in, help appears from out of nowhere. Some character we thought was lost or some clue we've forgotten snatches victory from defeat. It's too good to be true. You can hear the sniffles all throughout the movie theater.

The Bible is the true "too good to be true" story that we're meant to find ourselves in. Or, more accurately, lose ourselves in, so that we can find ourselves.

To understand the story of our lives, we need to understand the story of the Bible. That's what we're going to talk about in this chapter. But first we need to go back to the kitchen.

The ingredients may be prepped, but they're not dinner yet.

THEY'RE NOT DINNER YET

What is waiting for us when we walk back into the kitchen? Piles of chopped meat, vegetables, spices, and other ingredients all over the counter. What's for dinner? It's hard to tell. It could be spaghetti.

Two things are obvious at this point. The first is that we can't eat this stuff yet. Oh, we might be able to snack on a few of the ingredients, but it's not yet a meal. The flavors need to come together, mingle for a while, and then pass the taste test. The final meal is always more than the sum of its parts. That's true for Bible study too.

---

1. J. R. R. Tolkien, "On Fairy Stories," *The Tolkien Reader* (New York: Ballantine Books, 1966), 85–86.

The second thing that's obvious is that prep work takes a lot of time but doesn't give instant results. Can't we just skip this step? Is it worth it?

Let's tackle these questions together, then move on to step two.

Can We Skip Step One?

Prepping the ingredients is hard work, and it's not very glamorous. That's why we never see prep work on the cooking shows. All we see is the celebrity chef keeping up a stream of chatter while he adds one pre-chopped and premeasured ingredient after another to his sizzling sauté pan. But without his prep team, he wouldn't have a show.

They *never* skip this step; they just don't show it.

Cooking blogs agree that prep work—or *mise en place*,[2] the French term meaning "putting everything in place"—is not only an essential step in the process of cooking, it's also a mindset. It prepares you, as well as preparing the meal. Skipping the prep work means chopping as you go, finding out that you're missing the third ingredient, digging through your pantry for a substitute, and burning the onions so badly that you set off the fire alarm.

That said, experienced cooks also learn how to tweak this step for different occasions.[3] They know when to combine ingredients or how to take a legitimate shortcut. They know how to maximize counter space and minimize dirty dishes. Beginner cooks can expect to get better at the prep work.

The same thing is true for the prep work of Bible study. It's hard work and not very glamorous. But it's also essential. Obviously, the finished product depends on it. But, even more importantly, it changes your mindset. It trains you to be observant.

2. G. Stephen Jones, "Mise En Place" *The Reluctant Gourmet* (blog), July 17, 2012, http://www.reluctantgourmet.com/mise-en-place/.

3. See Emma Christensen, "Basic Technique: Mise En Place," *The Kitchn*, March 2, 2009, http://www.thekitchn.com/basic-technique-mise-en-place-77788, which is followed by 33 comments from experienced cooks talking about how they modify their prep work.

That's why it's worth it, to answer the second question.

It's hard work to observe the facts without jumping to interpretation. I still find that to be true. Most of us tend to editorialize or personalize too quickly. For example, we read about David and Goliath and make the story all about the virtues of David's faith—editorializing. Or we focus on Goliath and wonder what giants we're facing in our lives today—personalizing. By doing that, we don't see what's actually there in the chapter.[4]

With training, we realize that we've jumped ahead of ourselves, and we go back for a second look.

What Do I Need for Step Two?

We've finished step one (prep) and are ready for step two: cook. What do we need for that? More to the point, how does this stuff become dinner?

First, we need to snack on what we've already studied. If you were slicing apples for a pie, you'd probably eat a few slices before you started baking it. Our first step—prep, or observation—yields plenty of tasty morsels to feed our souls.

Second, to cook, we need one more tool and one last ingredient. I call them

- the *big pot*, and
- the *missing ingredient*.

The big pot is the whole story of the Bible. We need to place the story that we have prepped—as well as our own story—into the big story of the Bible.

---

4. What we see as a battle between individuals is actually a battle between two champions who represent their entire nations. The text makes it clear. David (the anointed king) isn't fighting a personal giant; he's fighting for Israel in the name of the God of Israel. It's a conflict between kingdoms. This observation changes how I will interpret and apply that familiar story.

The missing ingredient is Jesus. Every page of the Bible is ultimately about him. Every page pictures him or points to him or points back to him. Without Jesus, our meal won't taste right. He is the "bread from heaven" (John 6:32). He is the "honey from the rock" (Ps. 81:16).

THE BIG POT

Have you ever been cooking for company when the person called and asked if he or she could bring along a few extra guests?

Fortunately, you have just enough ingredients to double the recipe. Everything fits into the pot, just barely. You cover it and leave it on low heat. Before long, strange noises are coming from the kitchen. You run into the room and see the pot bubbling over. What a mess.

You're going to need a bigger pot to feed all those people.

A Big Enough Pot

The whole Bible is the only pot big enough to contain all the ingredients of every story that we study. It's even big enough to contain the ingredients of our lives.

God is like a master chef, and the Bible is his cookbook. He creates all of his recipes using the same four ingredients:

- What happens
- God
- People
- The relationship between God and people

Under his skillful hand, every page of his cookbook yields a distinct dish, so that his book overflows with astonishing variety. At the same time, every recipe bears the same characteristic flavor that permeates the whole book. We might call it a "culinary theme." And this theme is an important part of cooking! Winston Churchill is reputed to have growled his disapproval of a dessert that lacked this kind of inner cohesiveness: "Take away this pudding; it has no theme."[5]

What, then, is the theme of our big pot? It's the distinctive flavor of a pursuing God and how far he will go to bring us back to himself. The ingredients in the big pot are the same ingredients we've been examining in the dish Philemon: God, people, the relationship between them, and what happens.

God is like a great King.

The *people*—we—are his subjects, created not just to submit to him, but to rule the earth with him under his leadership.

The *relationship between us* was meant to be far more than that of a King ruling his subjects. We were created in his image, like children who look like their father.

The *relationship between us* was based on a solemn agreement between God and man, a covenant.

The *primary culinary theme*, then, is about a King who makes a covenant.

What happens? Well . . .

Once upon a Time

Once upon a time there was a great and good King. At the beginning of our story he creates a kingdom—a place and a people to flourish under his rule. The place—a garden—is both beautiful and abundant, meant to nourish both the souls and the stomachs of his people.

Next he creates the first people to live in his kingdom—a man and a woman—and places them in the garden to enjoy and cultivate it. They have been created in the King's image—great,

5. See "Personal Life," *The Churchill Centre*, last accessed August 10, 2016, http://www.winstonchurchill.org/resources/reference/faq/personal-life.

though not as great as he, and good, though not as good as he, for their goodness has not yet been tested and found pure.

The King intends not just to rule his subjects from far away, but to draw near and relate to them personally. Because of his infinite greatness and blazing goodness, he can't just hang out with them. This is not a casual relationship; they are not equals. So he creates a meeting ground by setting up a covenant between them. The terms of that agreement are this, "If you obey me, there will be peace between us. We will be allies. Even more, we will be friends."

The covenant guards both his majesty and their frailty. It secures the common ground where their friendship can flourish.

In the garden only one command is given: "Don't eat the fruit from the tree in the middle of the garden." Breaking it would not only be an act of rebellion against the King, it would break the treaty and end the relationship.

In one terrible moment the man disobeys (for he was the one held responsible), and the covenant is completely broken. The man and his wife are exiled. Soon their family is hit with further chaos and tragedy. Each one tries to be his own king, making his own laws, calling good evil and evil good.

Society disintegrates.

Dramatic Tension

A friend of mine started reading the Bible because someone told her that she should. She was shocked by it. "There are so many messed-up people in the Bible! I thought they were better back then, closer to the beginning. I thought we were the ones who messed everything up."

What she didn't realize was that, when the first rule was broken, the covenant was broken. It was a covenant of law. The relationship between the King and his people depended on both sides keeping the rules.

When we failed to keep our side of the agreement, things fell apart immediately and dramatically. Cut off from a relationship with our King and Creator, we plummeted into the worst sorts of evil. There was no golden age. Hatred led to murder in the very first generation.

But, inexplicably, God seemed to give us second (and third, and fourth . . .) chances. The broken covenant wasn't the end of the story. God's rule had been broken, but he nevertheless began extending his relationship to a whole string of people—Noah, Abraham, Isaac, Jacob, Moses, David. It seemed like he was giving them a free pass. How could God do that? Did he no longer care about his rules?

This is the dramatic tension in the whole story of the Bible. It points to a missing ingredient.

THE MISSING INGREDIENT

Without the missing ingredient, the dish won't taste right.

You try to make your grandmother's mashed potatoes for Thanksgiving, but they just don't taste the same. You followed her recipe, but something seems to be missing. So you give her a call and ask her about it. Sure enough, she forgot to tell you about the garlic.

Our taste buds help us with Bible study, too. The psalms tell us that the Bible, specifically the Law of God, is supposed to taste sweet, "sweeter also than honey and drippings of the honeycomb" (Ps. 19:10). That was David's experience.

But it's not always my experience. Sometimes the Bible tastes bland or bitter. When it's bland, I neglect it. When it's bitter, I swallow it like medicine. Why do I not taste the sweetness that David did?

Because something's missing.

Let's pick up our story again and look for it.

What's Missing?

Though the darkness is deep, it isn't the whole story. There has been hope all this time. You see, the King (with his Son) came up with a rescue plan, announced in barest terms to the devastated man and woman so that they would have hope in their exile. His plan has been foretold not once but many times. Those who take the prophecies seriously keep watch for the mysterious rescuer.

Hopes rise, only to fall again as hero after hero fails.

Finally, after years of silence and waiting, the King's Son appears on the scene. His words ring with authority. His miracles shout power. Is he the One, the promised Rescuer? Surely now he will crush the Serpent's head!

But, appallingly, no one recognizes him. The King's Son is opposed, and finally—unbelievably—murdered. The story threatens to end in tragedy.

Then it turns. The King's Son didn't come to reign. He came to fulfill the covenant by his life and death, mending it once and for all. Having completed his quest, he rises from death as proof that a new covenant is now in place. The story turns suddenly from tragedy to comedy. The King's Son ascends to his throne and waits until crowds of sons and daughters from every continent sign the new covenant and enter the kingdom.

We wait for the final act, when the King's Son will return and restore the kingdom at last to a greater goodness than it had in the beginning.

Do-It-Yourself Project

When we read our Bibles, we see the same thing my friend did. Life outside Eden is full of suffering and sin. We feel the dramatic tension. The covenant is broken, so God must be mad, but he doesn't always act mad. Sometimes he blesses the people in the story anyway. What's up with that?

We try to resolve the tension in the Bible story we're reading. We see a good character and figure that he or she must be the hero of this chapter. His or her good actions and faith must have earned the blessings that appear at this point on the timeline. After all, God rewards obedience, doesn't he?

We do this in our personal lives too. We know that God has high standards and that we don't always measure up. So we go to the Bible to find out how to please him and try our best to do what he says. Some days we do pretty well at obeying whatever rule we find, so we smile and wait for the blessings to come. Other days we don't do so well, so we cringe and wait for the curse to hit us.

We're always trying to mend the broken covenant from our side of the agreement. We think that's what the Bible stories are about. We think that's what our lives are about.

But we're wrong. Only one person was able to mend the broken covenant. Jesus, in his perfect obedience and atoning death, took the curse that was meant for us and earned the blessing of God's smile forever.

The surprise of the story is that God himself—Father, Son, and Spirit—is both the Maker and the Keeper of this covenant. It is a covenant of grace. Its blessings are now ours for free, through faith in the one who kept it for us: Jesus.

Interpreting any page of our Bible—Old Testament or New—without Jesus will make it taste bland or bitter or just plain wrong. The same is true when we interpret our lives.

The Bible without Jesus Does More Harm Than Good

Studying our Bibles without seeing Jesus in them will do us more harm than good. Does that surprise you? We often assume that Bible reading in itself is good. We may think that reading the Bible will please God. Or we may think that if we both read and obey the Bible, it will make us better people. But it won't—not without Jesus.

That's exactly what Jesus said to some of history's most diligent students of the Scriptures, the Pharisees. They loved God's Word, but they missed the point.

> You search the Scriptures because you think that in them you have eternal life; and it is they that bear witness about me, yet you refuse to come to me that you may have life. (John 5:39–40)

Now, no one knew the Scriptures like the Pharisees. They studied, memorized, scrutinized, and tried to obey them perfectly. Why? They thought that they could please God by their obedience. Their ancestors had been severely judged for their disobedience, so the Pharisees redoubled their efforts to avoid curses and earn God's blessings. They were determined to obey every law in as much detail as they could.

They were aiming for perfection because they wanted life. And they thought that they could find life in the Scriptures—in the law of Moses. But they had missed the point, and Jesus told them so: "If you believed Moses, you would believe me; for he wrote of me" (John 5:46).

Did Jesus' words produce a dramatic turnaround? Did the Pharisees suddenly run to the Scriptures and search them to find Jesus? No. Why not? Their pride was invested in their ability to save themselves by keeping the law. Compared to everyone around them, they were doing pretty well. You could say that they felt good about themselves. They rejected Jesus' words because they thought they were doing fine without him. Reading the Scriptures without Jesus fed their self-righteousness.

Scripture alone isn't the bread of life. Jesus is. And he wanted everyone to know it. In the very next scene recorded after his conversation with the Pharisees, he fed the five thousand so that he could tell the crowd, "I am the bread of life" (John 6:35).

The Bible with Jesus Is Sweeter Than Honey

When is our hunger satisfied? Not when we read our Bibles, but when we see Jesus there. He—who he is, what he came to do—is the missing ingredient. He completes our ingredient list. We throw *who he is* and *what he came to do* into the pot, then we watch how he turns the other four ingredients into a meal.

What happens? This is the action of the story. We often take the story's action and turn it into the action plan for our day. In fact, we often go to the Bible to find out what we need to do.

But the Bible isn't first about what we do. It's primarily about what Jesus did.

His every action accomplished the saving work of God. His work, not our work, is the focus of the action in the Bible. When we talk about "what happened" in the text we're studying, we're talking about what he did, not what we should do.

God. Jesus Christ is the Son of God, the second person of the Trinity. He is God made visible. We often long to see God, to have a personal encounter with him. Jesus' disciples wanted that too. "Whoever has seen me has seen the Father," he told them (John 14:9). As we learn to see Jesus in the passage, we will see God.

Jesus is God made audible. Many times we long to hear God speak to us. We look for a sign—a hawk in the sky, a white feather at our feet. We read our circumstances as if they were tea leaves. But God has already spoken to us, most clearly and finally, by his Son (Heb. 1:2). As we learn to hear Jesus in the passage, we will hear God speak to us.

Jesus shows us God.

People. Jesus is also the person whom God intended us to be. Because of the incarnation, we get to see our humanity fleshed out. We see the perfect integration of mind, will, and emotions under the rule of God. We see the beauty of holiness in human form.

Jesus is everything we should have been.

But he's not just the perfect image bearer. He's also our sin bearer. He is able to repair the damage that sin has done in each of us. He's our only hope for fulfilling our potential.

Jesus shows us what we will be when he has finished his work in us.

The relationship between God and people. Because Jesus is both God and man, he is the only one who can stand between us and join hands with both of us. The alienation caused by our disobedience is real. Only Jesus can reconcile us to God. He is the only Mediator between God and man.

How does he do it? Jesus' perfect life far surpassed the best efforts of the Pharisees. He obeyed from the heart. He kept the covenant of law given to Adam. He paid for the covenant of law broken by Adam and by us.

Jesus satisfied the covenant of law and turned it into a covenant of grace. It's his grace that makes Scripture taste sweet.

WHY WE NEED THIS

Why do you and I need to see Jesus as the missing ingredient whenever we do Bible study?

We're a lot like the Pharisees. We want to prove that we're good, even if our idea of goodness is different from theirs. Some of us prove it by saving the whales and eating vegan and feeding the homeless. Some of us prove it by saving babies and eating biblical grains and feeding the homeschooled.

We'd much rather save ourselves, thank you very much. We're slow to ditch our self-salvation project, because it feeds our pride. When it's going well, we're pumped and filled with the energy of ego-gratification. When it's going poorly, we either try harder or punish ourselves to save God the trouble.

Saving ourselves is the operating system we were born with. Overnight we default to it. Every day we need to reboot the good news that Jesus is our only Savior.

Here, in a nutshell, is our problem with Bible study: we turn to the Bible to reboot the gospel, but our operating system affects how we read it. In default mode, we don't see Jesus. Instead, we see more ways to save ourselves—through legalism or moralism.

Let's see how this might happen in our Philemon study.

Legalism

When we fall back on legalism, we take the laws and commands and try to obey them to become good or earn God's approval.

We read the book of Philemon, and one of the commands jumps out at us. Paul asks Philemon not just to forgive his runaway slave but to take him back as a brother. To go above and beyond the call of duty.

We want God to bless our day, so we try to think of a way to apply this. *I don't have any runaway slaves to forgive, so I guess I'll forgive the driver who cut me off in traffic yesterday.* We feel like our day is off to a good start.

Then we remember the rift between us and a friend. Former friend, that is. Just thinking about it makes us angry again. *I know, I know. I'm supposed to forgive her. But I'm so mad! Okay, I'll try to forgive. But be her friend again? No way!*

We slink away from our failure and imagine that the day has been jinxed.

But we don't need to earn God's blessings by our obedience. *Jesus already has.* Tasting his grace again helps us with today's bitterness. Since he's obeyed perfectly, we can run our race today, looking to him (Heb. 12:1–2).

Moralism

When we fall back on moralism, we look at every biblical character and see him or her primarily as an example to be followed.

We read Philemon and observe that Paul is imprisoned for his witness, yet he doesn't spend his time complaining about the rations or the rats. Instead he unselfishly cares about someone else's problems. It's astounding, really. He pours out his heart as if he has nothing else on his mind.

This letter costs him one of his best servants, too.

We see Paul's example and make a mental note. *I need to be more unselfish. Quit complaining about my life. Buck up and be like Paul.* The inspiration might get us through the day, and we end up feeling pretty good about it.

Or we might have a meltdown because our prison rations have been cut and the rats are taking over.

We don't need an example; we need a Savior.

Only when we see that all Scripture is really about Jesus does it take on the right flavor. We need Jesus to rescue us—and our Bible study too.

It's great to know that our hunger will be satisfied when we see Jesus on the page of our Bibles, but how do we do that?

To see Jesus, we need help—some legitimate shortcuts—which is the subject of our next chapter.

FOR REFLECTION AND DISCUSSION

1. Have you ever lost yourself in another story? What did you love about it?

2. The big story of the Bible is about a King who makes a covenant. What dramatic tension drives the plot forward? How is it finally resolved?

3. Why does interpreting the Bible without Jesus do more harm than good? How does it affect our understanding? Our application?

4. "Interpreting any page of our Bible—Old Testament or New—without Jesus will make it taste bland or bitter or just plain wrong" (p. 182). Why is that the case? Have you had that experience when reading the Bible or hearing God's Word preached?

5. How would you define moralism and legalism? What does your own struggle with them look like?

Ten

Shortcut

And their eyes were opened,
and they recognized him.
—Luke 24:31

Our challenge, then, is not to hack our way through
dense forest, but to discern the routes that the Bible's
Designer has already embedded in the landscape.
—Dennis Johnson, Walking with Jesus through His Word

My husband is a hands-on kind of guy.

When we got a sewing machine, he had to try it out. When we wallpapered the bedroom, he took the lead. When we decided to start baking our own bread, he was the first one in the kitchen.

I had found a recipe for no-knead whole wheat bread that looked promising for a beginner. This was in the days before bread machines and heavy-duty mixers, so not having to knead the dough was a plus.

My husband assured me that he'd have time between classes that day to whip up our first loaf. I left for the bus stop anticipating the smell that would greet me when I walked in the door ten hours later.

He glanced at the clock and got busy. There would be just enough time to proof the yeast and mix the dough before he had to leave for class. It could rise while he was gone. He checked the clock again. Barely enough time.

"Add the yeast to 1½ cups of lukewarm (80ºF) water."

He stopped. Where was our thermometer? Did we even have one? He poked through a few drawers and then decided that maybe he should try a shortcut. It couldn't be that hard to test the water's temperature—it was probably like bathwater. So he ran the tap until it felt right, added the yeast, and went in search of the rest of the ingredients.

Hours later I walked into the apartment nose first. Yes! I floated into the kitchen on the scent of warm, fresh bread and then stopped, puzzled. No bread in sight.

"Honey, where's the bread you made?"

"It didn't rise . . ." he called from the other room, ". . . but I think we can use it as a doorstop."

TAKING SHORTCUTS

This chapter is about learning to use shortcuts to see Jesus in our Bibles. But how do we know if a shortcut is a good one? How do we know it won't spoil the recipe like my husband's did? Are shortcuts even a good idea in the first place?

Who Needs a Shortcut?

Who needs a shortcut? The purists among us might roar, "*Nobody!*" But the fact is that we all need shortcuts to help us to fit all the things we need to do into the time we have. We're busy people, and we're always bumping up against our limits.

What we want to know is where we can cut corners without

sacrificing anything important. We don't have time for all the steps. We don't even understand why some of the steps are necessary. In the kitchen, for example, we might wonder:

- Do I really need to sift the dry ingredients together before I add them?
- Do I have to alternate between adding wet and dry ingredients to the batter?
- Can I use garlic out of a jar, instead of using fresh garlic?

Along the way, we learn that some shortcuts are a bad idea.[1] They don't work at all. Others sacrifice some of the quality but can be useful in a pinch. And some are truly legitimate. They save time, *and* they produce good stuff. The proof is in the empty pudding bowl.

America's Test Kitchen

How can we tell a good shortcut from a bad one without having to try them out for ourselves? Consult an expert. *America's Test Kitchen* is one resource that exists to help all of us amateur cooks.

In the PBS show, the cooks don't just write recipes: they test them. They don't just test them personally: they test them on ordinary cooks like you and me. They study how we use the very recipes they've written. The show's host, Christopher Kimball, explains,

> We bring people into our kitchen and watch people cook our
> recipes and send our recipes out by email, and we know that
> what people do with those recipes bears little resemblance to

---

1. My trial-and-error answers to these questions are *yes* (the sifting adds air and removes lumps, making these ingredients lighter), *yes* for the same reason as number 1 (a lighter finished product), and *no, not ever* (so find yourself a good garlic mincing tool)!

what we do with them. . . . For example, they will substitute ingredients with great abandon. They will never read the recipe ahead of time.[2]

Many of these substitutions and shortcuts produce disastrous results, like when one person substituted shrimp because he didn't have any chicken on hand. The problem was that the recipe called for forty minutes of cooking time. Shrimp can't handle that kind of heat.

Surprisingly, Kimball never blames the cook when his recipes fail. In his view, the failure is due to a flaw in the recipe, so he makes the appropriate changes. That's probably why people find the magazine that he founded, *The Cook's Illustrated Cookbook*, to be so useful.

His recipes aren't just tested by experts: they're tested by us.

Shortcuts to Jesus

The shortcuts I'm going to give you have been learned from the experts[3] and developed and tested over years in my own experience in personal study as well as in teaching women. Recently I sifted my shortcuts through the work of six scholars and preachers[4] to make sure I wasn't leaving out a major topic.

My categories avoid the specialized vocabulary of theologians in favor of everyday language. But the purpose is the same.

---

2. "Tried and True Tricks from 'America's Test Kitchen,'" *NPR*, December 7, 2011, http://www.npr.org/2011/12/07/143259669/tried-and-true-tricks-from-americas-test-kitchen.

3. My first exposure to seeing Jesus in the Old Testament came from Graham Goldsworthy's book *Gospel and Kingdom* in *The Goldsworthy Trilogy* (Milton Keynes, UK: Paternoster, 2001), which I read in 2006. My deepest exposure has come from Edmund Clowney and Timothy Keller, "Preaching Christ in a Postmodern World" (lecture series, Reformed Theological Seminary, Orlando, FL, 2002), which I accessed online at https://itunes.apple.com/us/itunes-u/preaching-christ-in-postmodern/id378879885?mt=10.

4. Timothy Keller, *Preaching: Communicating Faith in an Age of Skepticism* (New York: Viking, 2015), 256–58 (see note 2). Keller collates various ways to see Christ in the Bible from the works of Sinclair Ferguson, Sidney Greidanus, Graham Goldsworthy, David Murray, Gary Millar, and Bryan Chapell.

A shortcut has to match the purpose of the longer way it cuts around. It's not just about saving time. The shortcut has to bring you to the same final destination.

What's the final destination? Understanding the Bible according to the purpose of both its Divine Author and its human authors. Seeing Jesus is the way to do that, as we learned in the last chapter.

It's important to realize that each book of the Bible has not one but two authors: one human, one divine. The human author writes to a specific group of people in a specific time of history. The divine Author guides the human author's mind to ensure that what he writes is true and reliable for all time. The divine Author also insures that the smaller story is part of one big story arc from Genesis to Revelation.[5]

The purpose of both authors is to show that *God is the only Savior*, not in mind-numbing repetition but in mind-blowing variations on the theme, through all kinds of people and situations.

This means that "seeing Jesus" is not a clever game like "Where's Waldo?" It's also not a trick to pull out at Bible study so that we can impress our friends. And it's certainly not a test of our spiritual IQ to see how often we can get the right answer.

"Seeing Jesus" is more like seeing the life-giving Coast Guard boat race toward us as we flail in the ocean. We're drowning in life's demands, our own painful emotions, our recurring sins. We need to see our Savior so that we can grab him before we go under.

The following biblical themes are shortcuts to help us to see Jesus more quickly. Ask the Holy Spirit to open your eyes.

---

5. This is a simple explanation of a nuanced theological issue. A good summary of all the issues related to the nature of Scripture can be found in the Chicago Statement on Biblical Inerrancy, available online from the Center for Reformed Theology and Apologetics, accessed April 25, 2016, http://www.reformed.org/documents/index.html?mainframe=http://www.reformed.org/documents/icbi.html.

INTRODUCING EIGHT SHORTCUTS FOR SEEING JESUS

You've already prepped Paul's letter to Philemon. You've observed both God and the people carefully. Remember the short list in chapter 8 of things to look for when you are observing God? Remember the short list of character types that I introduced in that chapter, too?

While these are helpful ways to break down the passage, their most important role is to serve as shortcuts to find Jesus. You're hot on his trail! Here they are again, combined into one chart.[6]

God's	Man or Woman as
1. Character	5. Hero
2. Commands	6. Villain
3. Promises	7. Sinner
4. Mercy	8. Sufferer

10.1 Eight Shortcuts to Jesus

These are eight possible ways you can find Jesus in any part of your Bible. You may find more than one shortcut; don't expect to find all eight. If the passage contains several possible shortcuts, pick one for your focus.

Remember what's at stake. Jesus is our missing ingredient. Without him, we won't properly understand the meaning of the passage. That passage is in the Bible to point to Jesus, according to the Author's intention.

If we don't see Jesus, we won't taste the sweetness of the passage either. We might come away with legalistic or moralistic applications for our lives. But, when we see the saving purposes of God on the page, we see them more easily in our lives.

6. The charts in this chapter are also reproduced in Appendix A as a worksheet.

Let's look at these eight shortcuts. I'll define each one, give an example, and explain how it points to Jesus. Then we'll practice shortcutting on our own with the book of Philemon.

ILLUSTRATING SHORTCUTS 1–4

The first four shortcuts start with God and lead us to Jesus. We talked about our hunger to know God in chapter 1. Many of us, both inside and outside the church, long for an encounter with God. We hope that this is the place where we'll find the sense of peace and well-being that feels so elusive in our experience.

We turn to the Bible because we've been told that it's where we can find answers to our questions about God and our lives. But what we read often leaves us puzzled. How can we interpret the data we've collected? How can we know this God as he really is? How can this book help us?

The Book itself tells us how. The way to know God is through Jesus. "No one has ever seen God; the only God, who is at the Father's side, he has made him known" (John 1:18).

Let's see that truth in action through these shortcuts.

God's	Man or Woman as
1. Character	
2. Commands	
3. Promises	
4. Mercy	

10.2 Four Shortcuts from God to Jesus

1. Do I See a Character Quality of God in This Passage?

God's character traits—often called attributes—are revealed through his words and actions, just like ours are. Sometimes his character is seen in action, like when he was patient with all Moses' questions (Ex. 3:11–4:9). Sometimes it is named, like when the angels in Isaiah's vision chanted "holy, holy, holy" (Isa. 6:3).

A friend once remarked, "I have a hard time with God's holiness. It makes me feel like he is far away." When the prophet Isaiah saw a vision of God in his holy glory, he fell apart. He was overcome by a sense of his own sinfulness and desperation.

But an incident in the life of Jesus casts a different light on God's holiness. Jesus went up the mountain with his three closest disciples and was transfigured in front of them from ordinary flesh to brilliant light. They fell on their faces before his holy glory, just like Isaiah had. Then Matthew writes, "But Jesus came and touched them, saying, 'Rise, and have no fear'" (Matt. 17:7). He *touched them*. Jesus came to bear our sin so that he could bring God's holiness near.

All God's character traits are revealed most fully and finally in the life, death, and resurrection of Jesus Christ. He is "the image of the invisible God" (Col. 1:15), which means that he made the invisible God visible throughout his earthly life. Suddenly we see not just an attribute but a person standing before us. Jesus is the Image Bearer.

 When we see an attribute of God in the Bible, we can ask, *How does Jesus make this aspect of God's character visible?*

2. Do I See a Command from God Here?

God's commands—or laws—are the verbal expression of his character. They are good because he is good.

Many specific commands on the pages of the Bible help us to get along with each other: some protect property, some guide private behavior, some bring about social justice. They seem doable, until right smack in the middle of a long list we see this one: "You shall love your neighbor as yourself" (Lev. 19:18). We think, *That's beautiful. I want to live that way.* But we can't do it. If we're honest, we admit that God may be the Law Giver, but we are lawbreakers. It's crushing.

Until we see Jesus.

Jesus came to be the Law Keeper. "Do not think that I have come to abolish the Law or the Prophets; I have not come to abolish them but to fulfill them" (Matt. 5:17). He loved his neighbor as himself 24/7, including when he tried to get away for some rest only to be found by the crowds (Mark 6:31–34). When that happened, he didn't sigh with resignation. He had compassion on them. He didn't tolerate them. He loved them.

Because the Law Giver became the Law Keeper, the commands of God are no longer a threat. As John says, "his commandments are not burdensome" (1 John 5:3). We can look at each command through Jesus and see:

- the specific righteousness that he earned for us by obeying the command
- the beauty of his obedience to the command, which makes us want to obey it, too
- the confidence of a cleansed conscience that removes our fear about trying again
- the certainty of help from the indwelling Holy Spirit

When we see a command of God in the Bible, we can ask, *How does Jesus make this command beautiful, not crushing?*

3. Do I See a Promise of God Here?

God's promises are the expression of his character in future action. Every time we hear the words "I will" spoken by him, we are hearing a promise from the lips of the Promise Maker.

The problem is that many of the promises are conditional.

For example, take the Promised Land. God promised to lead Israel into a land where they would have everything they needed and not be slaves. But when the people came to the border, they let fear defeat their faith. So God let them all die, then took their children in.

That's sobering. What's going to keep us from spoiling all the precious and magnificent promises that he's made to us in the Bible?

Jesus. He is the Promise Keeper. Because he fulfilled all the conditions of faith and obedience, he guarantees that every promise of God will be fulfilled for us in its proper time. "For all the promises of God find their Yes in him" (2 Cor. 1:20).

When we see a promise of God in the Bible, we can ask, *How does Jesus guarantee the specific conditions of this promise?*

4. Do I See the Mercy of God Here?

God's mercy is his forgiveness and leniency for those who've offended him. Criminals plead for mercy when they have no options left. They quit presenting their case and throw themselves on the pity of the judge or jury. There's just one problem. Mercy flies in the face of justice. Does God sacrifice justice when he shows mercy?

Take David and Bathsheba. David committed adultery—and also murdered Bathsheba's husband in cold blood. Justice demanded the death penalty. That was the law. But when David confessed his sin, he was told, "You shall not die" (2 Sam. 12:13). How could God ignore his own law that day and show David mercy?

God didn't ignore justice. Instead, he took David's sin and placed it on Jesus when he hung on the cross. David's Old Testament faith looked ahead to the Promised One, Jesus, though David didn't know him by that name. When Jesus died in David's place, he satisfied—even vindicated—God's justice so that David could receive mercy. "But God, being rich in mercy . . . made us alive together with Christ" (Eph. 2:4–5).

Because of Jesus, God can be rich in mercy for all who abandon their case and plead for mercy from his hand.

When we see God's mercy in the Bible, we can ask, *How does Jesus satisfy God's justice so that God could show mercy here?* Here's a chart summarizing the first four shortcuts.

Do I see . . .	How does Jesus . . .	Verse
1. a character quality of God here?	make this aspect of God's character visible?	"He is the image of the invisible God" (Col. 1:15).
2. a command of God here?	make this command beautiful, not crushing?	"I have not come to abolish [the Law and the Prophets] but to fulfill them" (Matt. 5:17).
3. a promise of God here?	guarantee this promise?	"For all the promises of God find their Yes in him" (2 Cor. 1:20).
4. a mercy of God here?	satisfy God's justice so that God can show mercy here?	"But God, being rich in mercy . . . made us alive together with Christ" (Eph. 2:4–5).

10.3 Following Shortcuts 1–4

ILLUSTRATING SHORTCUTS 5–8

The second four shortcuts start with people and lead us to Jesus.

We talked about our hunger to know ourselves in chapter 1. The fact that we can live with ourselves all our lives and not understand ourselves is one of the deep mysteries of the universe. No amount of navel gazing or personality testing seems to solve it.

Where then should we go for help? Not to the self-help section in our local bookstores, but to the Bible. Even though the Bible is not primarily a book about us, it allows us to understand ourselves in God's presence.

God knows all of us because he created us. But in Christ he knows us in a different way—personally, intimately. "If anyone loves God, he is known by God" (1 Cor. 8:3). We know ourselves most truly when we know ourselves through the saving love of Jesus.

Let's see that truth in action through these shortcuts.

God's	Man or Woman as
	5. Hero
	6. Villain
	7. Sinner
	8. Sufferer

10.4 Four Shortcuts from People to Jesus

5. Do I See Man or Woman as Hero Here?

Heroes are the people we turn to for help. We need them to be good and to *do* good. Every election gives us the chance to pick a leader who we hope will turn out to be a hero. The Bible is full of heroes—good kings, faithful prophets, wise women, brave men.

Here's an example. Solomon was reputed to be the wisest man on earth, solving complex moral problems and leading the nation to the high point of its history. We often turn to his book of Proverbs to learn some of that wisdom and to take it with us into our day. But Solomon failed to live by his own words. His kingdom suffered for it.

I need someone greater than Solomon (and his proverbs) to make me wise. Jesus pointed to himself with the words, "Behold, something greater than Solomon is here" (Luke 11:31). Jesus lived wisely, died for my foolishness, and rose to become to me "wisdom from God" (1 Cor. 1:30).

Bible heroes are more than moral examples for us to follow. They point to Jesus. He is the True Hero—the true King, the faithful Prophet, the wise Man, the Good Shepherd, the faithful and wise Servant. Every hero in our Bibles will help us to see Jesus more clearly. Every heroic action will show us something about his saving work that we hadn't noticed before.

When we see a hero in the Bible, we can ask, *How does Jesus exceed this person's words, actions, or virtues?*

6. Do I See Man or Woman as Villain Here?

What is a villain? In any story, the villain opposes the hero primarily, though his actions also cause plenty of collateral damage. In the big story, villains are those who set themselves against God and his anointed—they are anti-Christ. We suffer from the actions of villains, not because they oppose us but because they oppose God. Think Hitler and Stalin. Think Herod and Saul.

When we see a villain, we're tempted to make his bad example the moral of the story. *How can I avoid being like this bad guy?* Instead, we should ask, *How is this villain against Christ? And how are Jesus and his way so much better?*

Take King Saul, who opposed David, God's anointed king. Saul plots and rages and deceives and hunts his prey. He will do anything to hold on to power. But David, who points to Jesus, endures patiently and entrusts himself to God. He doesn't pursue power or demand his rights.

But Jesus isn't just a better hero than David (see shortcut 5). Jesus is the Suffering Hero who defeats all God's enemies at the cross. He is also the Conquering Hero, who delays his return to judge so that his enemies have an opportunity to turn and live.

When we see a villain in the Bible, we can ask, *How are Jesus and his way much better?*

7. Do I See Man or Woman as Sinner Here?

Do we see a sinner or a sin jumping off the page of the passage we are reading? I don't mean a generic "we're all sinners" kind of sin but a pivotal sin that drives the action or changes the direction of the story. Think of Peter's denials. Think of David's adultery and murder.

Maybe we think, *I could never do that.* Or maybe we see ourselves in the mirror of their sin. What then? Instead of making the passage first about us, we need to let it point to Jesus. Every sin cries out for a Savior. Every sinner needs forgiveness.

For example, Peter denied Jesus three times because he didn't know his own weakness and refused to listen to Jesus' warnings (John 21:15–19). He wept bitterly over his sin. But after Jesus died and rose for Peter, he came to Peter and restored his call to follow. Not only would Peter be enabled to shepherd the church, he would also be enabled to follow Jesus all the way to death, as he had originally wanted to do.

Yes, Jesus forgave Peter, but he did more than that. He also transformed him into the man who God had created him to be.

Jesus shows us the extremes to which God will go to save us from ourselves. "For our sake he made him to be sin who knew no sin, so that in him we might become the righteousness of God" (2 Cor. 5:21). Jesus became my sin-bearer so that he could restore me to be a perfect image-bearer.

When we see a sinner in the Bible, we can ask, *How does Jesus bear this sin and its consequences away?*

8. Do I See Man or Woman as Sufferer Here?

Alongside sinners, there are sufferers in the Bible—innocent sufferers who are primarily victims of other people's sins. Job's story is the most famous example of undeserved suffering. Many other innocent sufferers are women. Their suffering troubles us. We feel the injustice of it.

How can we make sense of it?

Hannah was a woman who suffered the anguish of infertility. But unlike us, she also suffered the taunting other wife—an additional burden imposed by the culturally accepted system of polygamy. Year after year she cried out to God. In time God answered her prayer for a child. But he gave her more.

Hannah's prayer of thanksgiving was spoken by Mary centuries later to express her praise for the baby in her womb. Hannah's words pointed to a God who lifts up the lowly and feeds the hungry. Mary didn't yet know how perfectly Jesus would do that for her and for her ancestor Hannah. The mockery that Hannah had suffered would be borne by Jesus. He too would be mocked by his enemies. He would die barren, fruitless.

But Jesus' death would result in resurrection. He would give birth to a countless multitude.

Before we try to make sense of suffering, we must first let it point to Jesus. Jesus is the only truly innocent sufferer; he suffered and also died at the hands of sinners. He takes our suffering so seriously that he bore it on himself into the grave, then rose to redeem not just us, but also our suffering. He not only suffered for us, he suffers with us. When we suffer, he feels it.

So when we see a sufferer in the Bible, we can ask, *How does Jesus experience, endure, and redeem this suffering?*

Here's a chart summarizing the second four shortcuts.

Do I see ...	How does Jesus ...	Verse
5. man or woman as hero here?	exceed this person's words, actions, or virtues?	"Behold, something greater than Solomon is here" (Luke 11:31).
6. man or woman as villain here?	show that his way is much better?	"For I have no pleasure in the death of anyone, declares the Lord GOD; so turn and live" (Ezek. 18:32).

7. man or woman as sinner here?	bear this sin and its consequences away?	"For our sake he made him to be sin who knew no sin, so that in him we might become the righteousness of God" (2 Cor. 5:21).
8. man or woman as sufferer here?	experience, endure, and redeem this suffering?	"Although he was a son, he learned obedience through what he suffered" (Heb. 5:8).

10.5 Following Shortcuts 5–8

PRACTICING ON PHILEMON

Our eight shortcuts might not seem very short at this point! Fortunately, explaining them takes longer than using them. Let's do that together.

Look back at Philemon and your observations. Did you see any of our eight shortcuts? Take fifteen minutes to find them. Then ask, *How does Jesus fulfill each one I saw?*

Here's a quick summary of the shortcuts I discovered.

- *God's mercy.* God had mercy on Onesimus through Paul. Onesimus deserved punishment, even death, but he was given a useful life.
- *Hero.* Paul acted like a hero as he brought Onesimus to faith, sacrificially sent him back to Philemon, and sought to reconcile slave and master. And he did all this instead of throwing himself a pity party in prison.
- *Sinner.* Today's reader properly sees the evil of slavery, which makes us sympathetic to Onesimus, the runaway slave. However, under Roman law he was a lawbreaker, not just useless to his master, but costing him trouble and loss of income.

- *Sufferer.* Though Paul doesn't talk much about it, he is suffering as an old man in the chains and deprivations of a Roman prison.

Possible Takeaway

Perhaps the transformation of Onesimus caught your attention. You might be feeling useless, caught in the repetitive cycle of changing diapers or meeting deadlines. This shortcut seems promising for your struggle. You follow it like this:

God's mercy saved the slave's soul and also transformed him from useless to useful. Jesus made this astounding leniency possible by being the Servant who didn't run away but obeyed his Master all the way to the cross. He can make my service useful today too.

Or maybe you were convicted by Paul's heroic example. But instead of making resolutions to be less selfish, you ask, *How is Jesus the true hero here?* Then you reason:

Jesus forgave Paul and paid all his debts on the cross. Paul was transformed by this grace. That's why he can act like a hero and can urge Philemon to do the same. The same Jesus can work that in me too.

Maybe you're thinking about running away from your circumstances, like Onesimus did. But you stop to ponder how Jesus bore both your sins *and* their consequences away forever. You're filled with gratitude and strengthened to stay put.

Or you might identify with Paul's suffering, because you feel like you're in your own prison of sorts.[7] So you turn your thoughts to Jesus. He chose to be nailed to his prison, the cross, and he stayed until he died. He suffered for you. And now he suffers with you. You are not alone.

---

7. I have in mind things like the isolation of raising small children, the restrictions of long-term illness, the pain of repeated rejection in work or relationships. However, not all suffering is for a good cause. Some, especially in abusive situations, should be avoided or properly resolved.

My Takeaway

The first time I taught this material to a group of women, I dutifully sat down to study the passage and apply it to myself. At the time I was nursing a grudge against a friend.

Okay, Lord. I get it. I'm supposed to forgive my friend, just like Paul is asking Philemon to do. I'll give it another try. I don't know why this time will be any different, though.

Then the words in verses 17 and 18 caught my attention.

> So if you consider me your partner, receive him as you would receive me. If he has wronged you at all, or owes you anything, charge that to my account.

Suddenly, I had an aha moment. It was as though Jesus was speaking those words directly to me. "Rondi, do you consider me your partner? I know you do—you would receive me with open arms if I came to you. Receive her that way. But I also know that you feel offended. Her debt to you keeps getting in the way, so . . . *charge it to my account.*"

Faster than I could think it, Jesus impressed on me the invisible reality behind those printed words. His Spirit spoke them to my spirit in a flash. The power of his cross inserted itself into my story.

I was undone. I tearfully took my list of grudges and nailed it to his cross. That day the grip of my bitterness began to be broken.

Can't Quite See Him?

What if you can't quite see Jesus this time? Or you aren't sure you've got it right?

Don't be dismayed. Remember, Jesus is eager for us to find him. Hear his words to Mary Magdalene in the garden outside the empty tomb: "Woman, why are you weeping? Whom are you seeking?" (John 20:15).

Remember, a transforming sight of Jesus doesn't rest on your efforts alone. It is the work of the Holy Spirit. As you do your work, ask the Holy Spirit to open your eyes.

Remember, the word of God is always fruitful. If you forget, take a quick peek at Psalm 119. It gives us one hundred seventy-six ways that this is true.

God will make sure that his Word feeds you. You can count on that.

FOR REFLECTION AND DISCUSSION

1. How did this chapter motivate you to see Jesus?
2. How did this chapter help you to see Jesus?
3. Which shortcut makes the most sense to you?
4. Which is the hardest for you to grasp or use?
5. Do the fifteen-minute experiment on Philemon, using the shortcuts and the worksheet in Appendix A, to find Jesus for yourself.

Eleven

Eat

Your words were found, and I ate them.
—Jeremiah 15:16

Christians feed on Scripture. Holy Scripture nurtures
the holy community as food nurtures the human body.
—Eugene Peterson, Eat This Book

I pulled out my food processor and my biggest pot. I'd already washed the vegetables and spread them out on the counter—cabbage, onions, carrots, green peppers, celery, shallots, tomatoes, and garlic.

It was formidable.

I began shoving chunks of cabbage into the chute of the food processor. Within seconds the bowl was full. I dumped it into the pot and kept going. The celery went in next. I stopped when I got to the carrots and changed blades.

The pot was filling up. The onions, peppers, garlic, and shallots could be chopped together. *Shallots as well as onions? What's up with that?*

Just do it. Don't ask questions.

This was one of those recipes you had to follow to the letter, or it wouldn't work. It was the main dish for the amazing seven-day "Cabbage Soup Diet." My husband and I were counting on losing the seven to ten pounds promised by the promotional materials. Maybe more.

I kept adding vegetables to the pot until it was almost full. Then all I had to do was pour in vegetable broth and V8 juice, bring it to a boil, and let it simmer. Voila.

It won't be too bad, I convinced myself. *You get to have a baked potato on day 2. Bananas and milk on day 4. I love bananas.* Nothing else that day—but still, it was something to look forward to. My husband was excited about days 5 and 6, when you could eat meat.

And, of course, there was the cabbage soup. You could eat as much of that as you wanted. My pot held only eight quarts—I'd probably have to make a second batch.

WHAT'S ON THE TABLE?

It's time to eat. Finally. We've finished making our meal from Philemon, and now we get to sit down and eat it.

This chapter is about applying Scripture, but, in keeping with our food theme, we're going to call it *eating*.[1] That makes sense, doesn't it? When we apply Scripture, we take it in, and it changes us. When we apply food . . . well, a moment on the lips, forever on the hips.

The analogy between applying Scripture and eating it is more than a clever way of sticking with my metaphor. First, it's biblical: "Your words were found, and I ate them"; and, second, it's delightful: "and your words became to me a joy and the delight of my heart" (Jer. 15:16). We don't usually think of application as delightful.

1. See table 8.1 (p. 156).

If you're like me, you may be thinking, *Ah, yes, application. That's the part where God tells me what to do—how I need to change, grow, and do all the stuff he wants me to do for him today.*

We tend to think of application as our marching orders for the day. We might remember that we're supposed to be doers of the Word, not hearers only (James 1:22), so we're ready to roll up our sleeves and start doing. We'll add the divine to-do list to our own and get busy.

The food paradigm can help us here. The goal of cooking is eating. The goal of Bible study is feeding on Christ, not just finding application. It's a meal, not marching orders.

This is a meal that's meant to both nourish and change us.

Cabbage Soup or Comfort Food

What kind of meal are we sitting down to? Cabbage soup or comfort food?

When we're desperate for change, we want quick results. That's when we turn our Bibles into a spiritual cabbage soup diet. If we follow the rules, dot all the i's and cross all the t's, then maybe we'll finally lose that sinful habit that we've been struggling with.

So we go to the Bible looking for how-tos. We want to change ourselves or change our spouse or change our kids or change our world. A command of Scripture jumps up and down in front of us, promising to be the silver bullet for our particular problem of the day. "Do this and live! Do this and live!"

We add it to our to-do lists, right under "drink eight glasses of water," and we close our Bibles thinking, *Maybe this one will work.*

We may continue with this approach as long as we think it's working. If our spiritual scale shows that we're making progress, we stay motivated, adding new rules along the way. But if progress stops or reverses, suddenly we've had enough. We tear up the to-do list and pour out the rest of the cabbage soup.

What do we reach for then? Comfort food. This is the kind of food that's eaten for its psychological benefit more than its nutritional boost. It reminds us of home or stirs nostalgia for some golden moment in our lives. We love it because makes us feel better.

We turn the Bible into spiritual comfort food whenever we use it primarily as a mood booster. We wrap ourselves in its words for their emotional content. And we skip the parts that can't be used that way. We need a boost because we're worn out from trying so hard to please God and change ourselves. Can't he just give us a warm hug?

Of course, the Bible contains lots of comfort—real comfort, true comfort, strong comfort—but it's not like a plate of mac 'n' cheese (or bangers and mash) that remind us of Mom. It's not a book of empty words into which we can pour our own sentimental thoughts. That's just us trying to comfort ourselves, using someone else's words for our own purposes. The comfort won't last.

As the *New York Times* reported, "The emotional healing powers of comfort food may be overrated."[2] That's true for "comfort Scripture" too.

If the Scriptures aren't like cabbage soup or comfort food, what kind of a meal do they offer?

Food for My New Life

The meal we've just prepared for ourselves from Scripture is better than either option. It's food for life. True food for our new life. It's meant to nourish us (better than comfort food) and change us (better than cabbage soup). This meal is meant to do both, not one or the other.

Our new life is a life of faith. Our faith in God—Father, Son, and Spirit—needs to be nourished, so God gives us the

---

2. Jan Hoffman, "The Myth of Comfort Food," *New York Times*, December 15, 2014, http://well.blogs.nytimes.com/2014/12/15/the-myth-of-comfort-food/.

Scriptures with page after page of reasons that he can be trusted. This meal will nourish our faith in him.

Our new life is also a life of transformation. God doesn't give us a "get out of jail free" card and leave us to ourselves. He ushers us into the ultimate makeover, paid for by Jesus himself. This extreme makeover is better than any plan we might concoct to change the things we don't like about ourselves. It's God's plan to make us into the most glorious version of ourselves, a perfect reflection of his beauty.

This meal will both nourish and change us. How? Think about it. It takes some work to fix a meal, and it takes some time to sit and eat it. But we don't think about the food once we've finished—it is digested and metabolized without our help. We get up and get on with life.

In the same way, the Scriptures "enter our souls as food enters our stomachs, spreads through our blood, and becomes holiness and love and wisdom."[3]

Sustaining our life of faith is God's work. Transforming us is God's work. His Word is a way that he accomplishes this work in us. God uses his written Word to bring Christ not just near us but into us—and with him come all his benefits.

That's what we mean when we say that the Bible is a "means of grace"; we mean that it is a tool in God's hand—not ours—to do his redemptive work in our lives.[4] This meal that you've made is *his effective tool* to nourish and change you.

After years of studying, preaching, and translating the Scriptures, Eugene Peterson concludes,

3. Eugene H. Peterson, *Eat This Book: A Conversation in the Art of Spiritual Reading* (Grand Rapids: Eerdmans, 2006), 4.
4. Westminster Shorter Catechism,
   Q: 88: What are the outward and ordinary means whereby Christ communicates to us the benefits of redemption?
   A: The outward and ordinary means whereby Christ communicates to us the benefits of redemption are, his ordinances, especially the Word, sacraments, and prayer; all which are made effectual to the elect for salvation.

Christians don't simply learn or study or use Scripture; we assimilate it, take it into our lives in such a way that it gets metabolized into acts of love, cups of cold water, missions into all the world, healing and evangelism and justice in Jesus' name, hands raised in adoration of the Father, feet washed in company with the Son.[5]

This meal fuels my life of faith, my acts of service, and my pursuit of change. I think of it as a three-course meal.

A Three-Course Meal

One year I decided to do a Christmas shopping marathon at the mall. I should have known better.

Armed with a long list, sensible shoes, and a few not-so-sensible friends, I set out to conquer. We had mapped out our campaign. We had laid out our list according to the layout of the stores. We'd researched the sales. Planned our budget. Gotten up ridiculously early.

But we'd forgotten to bring food.

Of course, the restaurants were more crowded than the stores, so we pushed the thought of food out of our minds. That is, until it forced its way back in. Suddenly, I realized I was ready to drop. I couldn't make one more purchase or carry one more package until I got some food in me.

I won't bore you with the wait for a table and the even longer wait for food. But when it finally came . . . oh my.

I took my first bite. *Oh, this is good. This is really good. I didn't realize how hungry I was.* "You gotta try this. These fries are amazing!" We helped ourselves to bites from each other's plates. We had to agree. It was amazing. All thoughts of shopping and lists and sales were gone.

5. Peterson, *Eat This Book*, 18.

My mental fog was beginning to dissipate. I got chatty between mouthfuls. "I think I need to change my plan and buy for my out-of-town family first. I saw a scarf in the last store that I think my sister would love. Why don't we start there after we finish our food?"

By the time we pushed back from the table, we felt so much better. Energy had returned. Resolve had strengthened. We were warrior women again, returning to our quest.

We had just eaten a three-course meal. One that delighted us, renewed our minds, and restored our strength.

The meal before you will do the same. I call it gospel praise, gospel perspective, and gospel power.

FIRST COURSE: GOSPEL PRAISE

Food delights me before it accomplishes anything else. So does Scripture when I see Jesus there.

Gospel praise comes from catching another glimpse of Jesus my Savior and being amazed at his beauty again. He's mine, and he's more wonderful than I remembered.

Gospel praise erupts when I hear the good news of his finished work again and realize that it's finished for me too. Not just in the past, but today.

Gospel praise flows when I get a fresh taste of God's grace and roll it around on my tongue to savor as mine today.

Gospel praise is the first course of my meal, because seeing Jesus in his saving work from yet another angle always produces worship. We can't help ourselves. We can linger here. We don't need to rush past this first course to get to the more important stuff. Why?

What about the Important Stuff?

The important stuff is happening right now. We are being nourished and changed on the spot.

Whenever we "taste and see that the LORD is good" (Ps. 34:8), worship is our first response. The personal experience of his goodness—tasting and seeing—captures our imagination and causes us to say, "Wow! You gotta taste this. It's amazing!"

In that moment we find that:

- God is the center of our attention (we're not)
- God is the center of our affection (our idols aren't)
- God is the satisfaction of our appetite (our cravings aren't)

In worship God turns our attention away from our usual obsession: us. With one stroke he topples all our other gods[6] so that they lie scattered and broken in pieces all around us. We can see how useless they are. With one taste of his eternal goodness, he eliminates all our cravings for spiritual junk food.

Best of all, God exposes the Serpent's lie and proves, once again, that he is good, delivering a deathblow to our greatest temptation: doubting his goodness.[7]

That's why the meal must begin here, with savoring God's saving goodness. Worship is the first and best response to the gospel. It will lead to all the rest.

> Jesus' salvation is a feast, and therefore when we believe in and rest in his work for us, through the Holy Spirit he becomes real to our hearts. . . .
>
> This makes all the difference. If you are filled with shame and guilt, you do not merely need to believe in the abstract concept of God's mercy. You must sense, on the palate of the heart, as it were, the sweetness of his mercy.[8]

---

6. I explored the topics of idolatry and spiritual junk food in chapter 5.

7. The ancient lie—doubting God's goodness—was introduced in chapter 1 and explored in chapter 6.

8. Timothy Keller, *The Prodigal God: Recovering the Heart of the Christian Faith* (New

Worship arises when we taste Christ. That taste begins to nourish and change us.

A Business Trip

Let's say you're getting ready to leave on a business trip. Your mind is full of the thousand details you have to finish before you take off. You still need a dog sitter and a ride to the airport. You're also anxious about flying. Plus, you'll be traveling with your boss, who never seems satisfied with your performance.

Despite these pressures, you decide to sit down and finish your study of Philemon.

You look back through the letter, remembering that it's about Paul, Onesimus, and Philemon. In fact, the first time you read it, Philemon actually reminded you of your boss. You could imagine why Onesimus ran away. But now that you've seen that Jesus is at the center of the story, you're curious about how the whole thing applies to you.

I've got lots going on, Lord. What do you have for me here?

This time the word *refresh* catches your attention. You hadn't noticed it before. Paul uses the word twice. Apparently Philemon wasn't such a bad guy. He refreshed people: "The hearts of the saints have been refreshed through you" (Philem. 1:7). Now Paul wants Philemon to do the same for him: "Refresh my heart in Christ" (Philem. 1:20).

In Christ? Oh. The love that Philemon showed to the believers around him, that love came from Jesus. His love was a response to Jesus' love for him. The love of God in Christ Jesus is so great that it changes people so that they refresh others.

It changes me too. So. I. Can. Refresh. Others. Wow.

He *loves* me. He loves *me*. He loves me! *If Jesus loves me, I'm confident that he will give me everything I need.*

York: Riverhead Books, 2008), 121–22.

You're ready for your trip.

The gospel results in praise when I taste Christ. "Oh, taste and see that the LORD is good!" (Ps. 34:8).

SECOND COURSE:
GOSPEL PERSPECTIVE

Food dissipates my mental fog so that I can think clearly again. The Scriptures do that too, by renewing my mind and giving me gospel perspective.

What do I mean by gospel perspective? I mean that the gospel causes me to see the world differently, through the eyes of the God who sent his Son to rescue sinners. It changes my view of myself and of the people around me. It also changes my view of my circumstances.

Gospel perspective means that I begin to have the mind of Christ. When I see myself and the people around me through Jesus-colored glasses, I realize that we're all sinners in need of a Savior. I become more patient with them, even with the child who's pushing my buttons. I become more hopeful about them, even with the boss who always criticizes my performance. God can work in anyone, even me.

I begin to have the wisdom of Christ too. When I sit down with my Bible, I come with my list—hungers, questions, problems, needs. When I get up, the list may look very different. I sit down worried about my daughter's most recent report card. I get up realizing that I was sharp with her yesterday when she showed it to me. I go to apologize and pray with her.

Mental Health

I need the gospel perspective that Scripture gives me to keep from going crazy. So often I get myself worked up over everything I'm worried about. I lose perspective—everything seems terribly important, and I have no idea how to deal with it all. My tendency is to run in all directions at once, trying to fix things until I crash and burn.

Instead I need to run to Jesus. When I set aside my concerns long enough to listen to his Word, I'm amazed at the perspective he gives. What I thought was terrible looks different from his perspective. What I thought was so important when I sat down turns out to be not so necessary. What I thought was optional turns out to be important to him. Maybe it's taking cookies to that neighbor. Maybe it's calling my mother.

Gospel perspective is one way that God nourishes us through his Word. We sit down scattered. We get up collected. We sit down confused. We get up with greater clarity. We sit down heavy-hearted. We get up comforted. We sit down crazy. We get up in our right minds.

A Change of Mind

Let's say you're a mom who's become very exasperated with one of your children—the child you find hard to like, much less to love. She's stubborn and not very communicative. You're easygoing and a talker. You've been nagging her about how she spends her time after school, wanting her to get out and be more social, but she insists on coming home and spending hours in her room.

You're thinking about playing your trump card: making her join an after-school club. You're just trying to figure out which privilege you'll take away if she doesn't. She's due home from school soon, so you sit down to finish your study of Philemon.

I'm going to talk with her as soon as she walks in the door. You've got to change her, Lord!

You take another look at Philemon, trying to calm your mind. This time you notice how Paul talks to Philemon. He doesn't order him to take back his runaway slave, Onesimus. Instead, he *appeals* to him. Why? Because Paul expected God to be at work in Philemon through Christ. Paul had the authority to order him, but in love he appealed to him instead.

This changes your perspective. God is the one who is at work in your daughter. What a thought! Maybe you should try appealing to her. *How does Paul put it?* "Yet for love's sake I prefer to appeal to you" (Philem. 1:9). Then you realize that you'd *rather* command your daughter than appeal to her. The problem isn't with her—it's with you. Your love has cooled. You've become hard-hearted. You're the one who needs to change.

Before you know it, you're tearfully confessing before God your lack of love for your daughter.

The perspective of the gospel has changed your mind. That's what Paul meant when he said, "Be transformed by the renewal of your mind" (Rom. 12:2).

THIRD COURSE: GOSPEL PROVISION

Just as food strengthens my body, God's grace strengthens my heart. The Scriptures are a pantry stocked with grace, from Genesis to Revelation.

That's why gospel provision is the third course of our three-course meal. We're not meant to live the Christian life by Christian principles. We're meant to live it by Christ. His finished work has thrown open the door to God's storehouse of grace. Inside is every resource that you and I need for today.

That's what Paul meant when he wrote to the believers in Philippi, "My God will supply every need of yours according to his riches in glory in Christ Jesus" (Phil. 4:19).

That's great news for all of us weak people. We don't need Christian principles or five tips for a better life or ten steps to a better me. We need Christ. His gospel tells us what God has done for us. And then it goes one step further.

Christ's gospel tells us what God is *continuing* to do *in* us through the work of his Son and the gift of his Holy Spirit.

God at Work

Let's face it. We come to God's Word utterly preoccupied with ourselves. Our needs are arm-wrestling with each other for first place. It's an act of faith to set them aside for a moment so that we can focus on what God has to say to us.

God has been at work while we've been studying. He's helped us to pay attention; he's shown us Jesus; he's turned this text into food. We're tasting his goodness and seeing more clearly, but before we get up, he has one more thing for us.

He's going to give us strength for the life that we're returning to.

The Christian life looks ordinary, but it's utterly supernatural. Our daily work includes resisting the Devil, loving our enemies, fleeing temptation, and doing good to all. Humbly, of course, and without any expectation of thanks or praise. I need God's assurance that everything he's asking me to do, he will help me to do.

Gospel provision is God's continuous supply of grace through Jesus Christ in as many shapes and sizes as I need. There's some of it on the page in front of me.

I Can't Do This!

Let's say you've been going through a period of physical and emotional suffering. Even though these should be "the best years of your life," you've found yourself hemmed in by pain and weakness, and now by fears and discouragement too.

You came down with pneumonia over a year ago, and it caused your asthma to flare up. The steroids that the doctor gave you made you gain weight. You still have trouble breathing and have begun to sleep poorly. On top of that, your seasonal migraines have returned.

You feel trapped, imprisoned inside your house, your pain, your fears. You feel useless. Cut off from normal life. Isolated. Tired of asking for help and not being able to give in return.

You want to quit, but instead you finish your study of Philemon. You look over the letter one more time.

I can't do this, Lord. I can't keep going. What have you got for me here?

This time the description of Onesimus gets your attention, "Formerly he was useless to you, but now he is indeed useful to you and to me" (Philem. 1:11). This sentence is an aside from Paul, but it's front and center for you. *That's quite a transformation. Here he is, still a slave,* you think, *still a runaway, but he's already useful to his master. And not just to his master, but to Paul and to God.*

Not only that, but you also see that Paul is useful too, even from within the walls of his prison. Prison didn't define him; Christ did. God brought Onesimus to him. He bore fruit without leaving his house.

You're stunned. *God did this in them. Can he do the same in me?* You're feeding on gospel provision. Hope begins to flicker. Your prayers change. You renounce the lie of uselessness and get up to serve Jesus within the walls of your home.

The gospel includes God's provision through Christ for all our needs. "My God will supply every need of yours according to his riches in glory in Christ Jesus" (Phil. 4:19).

FOOD FOR THE ROAD

Let's recap this chapter. The last step in our Bible study is to feed on the good news of Jesus in the passage we have studied. When we do, he comforts us, nourishes us, and changes us so that our emotions, thoughts, and actions become fueled and transformed by his grace.

Here's a summary of our three-course meal.[9]

Eat: Feeding on the Gospel	Question	Verse
Gospel Praise	How is Jesus beautiful and how is his work wonderful to me today?	"Oh, taste and see that the LORD is good!" (Ps. 34:8).
Gospel Perspective	How does his gospel change the way I look at my life today?	"But be transformed by the renewing of your mind" (Rom. 12:2).
Gospel Provision	How will God provide for me today through Jesus?	"And my God will supply every need of yours according to his riches in glory in Christ Jesus" (Phil. 4:19).

11.1 Feeding on Christ

Leftovers

I love leftovers. They make for easy snacks to bag and take with me when I leave the house. The hard work of prepping and cooking is over. Leftovers are pure bonus. I bag some cut-up cantaloupe for a mid-morning snack. A serving of last night's mac 'n' cheese goes in a box for my lunch. A handful of trail mix will get me through the afternoon. I'm not going to go hungry.

You've done the hard work. Now take some of the leftovers into your day. Grab a sticky note or an index card and write down the one verse that helped you most today. Then take it with you. Stick it on your dashboard. Put it by your kitchen sink or next to your bathroom mirror.

When it catches your eye, read it again. It will bring back the flavor of the whole meal.

9. This chart is reproduced in Appendix A as a worksheet.

Make Mine to Go

Another way to make Scripture portable is to *memorize* it. I find it much easier to memorize something that I've studied and understood, rather than a verse out of context. It has already become meaningful to me. The effort to memorize it feels worth it.

The advantage of memorizing is that I have it with me at odd times when I need it and can't look it up: at night, when I don't want to get up or turn on the light and my mind wanders into fear or despair; during the day, when I'm driving and my mind dabbles with temptation or rebellion.

We're also encouraged to *meditate* on Scripture. The blessed man is the one who delights in God's law and "meditates [on it] day and night" (Ps. 1:2). However, we often think of meditation as reserved for spiritual superheroes or those who want an A+ on their spiritual report cards. So we excuse ourselves and figure we'll get to it someday.

But meditation is for all of us. It's the way we stay sane and strong and even joyful throughout our marathon days.

I found a great takeaway verse for meditation the other day in 2 Kings. I was reading about Naaman, the captain of Syria's army, who had leprosy. His Jewish servant girl told him to go to Israel so the prophet could cure him. The leper traveled to Israel but went to the king instead of the prophet, saying, "I've come to be cured of leprosy."

The king of Israel knew that he couldn't deliver, so he tore his clothes and said, "Am I God, to kill and to make alive, that this man sends word to me to cure a man of his leprosy?" (2 Kings 5:7).[10]

I love that. "*Am I God?*" Rhetorical question! Yet it covers so much ground.

---

10. In the context, the king's cry was a cry not of faith but of despair. However, for me it became a cry of faith, helping me to praise God, gain perspective, and see his provision that day.

So I took it into my day. Whenever I felt overwhelmed by people's demands, I would think, "*Am I God* that you would expect me to _____ (fill in the blank)?" Then I would say to myself, "Of course I'm not! Help, Lord!"

Memorizing and meditating go hand in hand as one more way to feed on the finished work of Christ. They bring the Scriptures into our minds long after we've closed our Bibles.

They remind us that the finished work of Christ will finish its work in you and me.

FOR REFLECTION AND DISCUSSION

1. "The goal of Bible study is feeding on Christ, not just finding application" (p. 211). How would you describe the difference between those two things?
2. Have you ever turned the Bible into cabbage soup or comfort food? What does it mean to see it as a "means of God's grace" instead?
3. "Worship is the first and best response to the gospel" (p. 216). How does worship both nourish and change us?
4. Use Philemon Worksheet #3, found in Appendix A, to look at Philemon again and come up with your own application of the book.
5. Pick the verse from Philemon that became most helpful to you along the way. Write it out and take it into your day.

Twelve

Share

*Philip ran to him and heard him reading Isaiah
the prophet and asked, "Do you understand
what you are reading?" And he said,
"How can I, unless someone guides me?"*
—Acts 8:30–31

*The Christian needs another Christian who speaks
God's word to him . . . The Christ in his own heart
is weaker than the Christ in the word of his brother.*
—Dietrich Bonhoeffer, Life Together

It was Sunday night, and I was spent. Monday loomed, and I already felt overwhelmed.

"What's for dinner, Mom?" That question, so innocent, put me over the top.

"Nothing! You're on your own!"

"Really? Cool."

I hadn't been expecting that response, but I pulled myself together and took charge of the situation. "Yes—from now on, Sunday evening is 'every man for himself' night. You three are old enough to figure something out."

My oldest child eyed me suspiciously. "Do you have to OK what we choose?"

"Nope."

She smirked and headed straight for the freezer. Pulling out the carton of leftover mint chocolate chip ice cream, she turned and held it defiantly in front of her like a shield. I shrugged. "Go ahead." Moments later she headed to her room where she kept her private stash of candy.

Meanwhile, our son dragged a chair over to the counter and began making popcorn. Apparently he had done this before. The youngest managed to find the sugary cereal I'd hidden behind the unsweetened Cheerios and poured herself an enormous bowlful. They went off to finish their game of Battleship.

My husband raised his eyebrows. "Me too?" I nodded. He grabbed the leftover pizza from lunch and made a beeline for the TV to turn on the Steelers game.

I looked around the empty kitchen. "That was too easy. I hope they don't expect this every night."

EATING ALONE

It's astonishing how quickly family dinnertime devolves into "every man for himself night" at the slightest encouragement.

Why is that? Certainly individual preferences play into it. ("Mom, I told you yesterday that carrots are one of the three foods I don't like. *You said* I could have three." "Yes, and I also told you that you can't keep changing them every week. Eat your carrots.") Time pressure can also squeeze a shared meal right out of the schedule. The piano lesson bumps up against volleyball practice, which leads right into Girl Scouts. Eating alone is easier. It's our default mode.

Then why do we instinctively resist default mode and fight to preserve family meals? Even if we can't articulate the reason, we sense that they're important. Shared meals take work, but they also bring greater benefit than simply filling our stomachs.

The family meal is equally important for our spiritual diet. In this chapter, we'll go from "me" to "we" in our quest to feed on Jesus in the Scriptures, and we'll unpack why it matters.

Up until now, we've focused on "me and my Bible." We've been training ourselves to recognize when our souls are hungry and to open our Bibles to look for food. We've been learning that food—Jesus and his saving work—can be found in some form on every page. We've been practicing how to prep, cook, and eat it, alone.

Eating alone is necessary and good, but it's not enough. Feeding on Christ is also meant to be a shared meal, prepared and served by my pastor, eaten together with my church, and taken with me to share with others.

Solo Eating—Two Problems

Regular shared meals go against the grain of our culture. Eating alone has become the American thing to do,[1] but it's also on the rise in Europe. Almost half of all meals—at home or out—are eaten alone, according to the Food Marketing Institute's 2014 grocery industry survey.[2]

The trend toward solo eating affects us all. I'm right there with the rest, packing food for the day so that I can eat in my car or on the job or in a coffee shop. Meanwhile, the culture around me is quickly adapting to help me to do it better.

Eating alone is changing how grocers stock their shelves and how restaurants treat their customers. It's spawning a new

1. Roberto A. Ferdman, "The Most American Thing There Is: Eating Alone," *Washington Post*, August 18, 2015, https://www.washingtonpost.com/news/wonkblog/wp/2015/08/18/eating-alone-is-a-fact-of-modern-american-life/.
2. Food Marketing Institute, U. S. Grocery Shopper Trends 2015 Executive Summary, accessed August 11, 2016, http://www.fmi.org/docs/default-source/document-share/fmitrends15-exec-summ-06-02-15.pdf, p. 10.

fleet of takeout-only establishments that deliver food just like the pizza man but with far more variety. In Amsterdam, it has even birthed Eenmaal, the first-ever eat-alone restaurant, filled exclusively with tables for one.[3]

You may agree that this trend is real, even that you're part of it, but what does it mean? It points in two directions: first to our disconnectedness and second to our individualism. Our disconnectedness is a problem that calls for compassion. Our individualism is a choice that calls us to consider.

Sometimes we eat alone because we've become disconnected from others through divorce or sickness or aging or other aspects of our broken world. In this case, eating alone is not so much a personal preference as a problem that's been forced on us, together with scanty portions and poor nutrition.[4]

But sometimes we eat alone because we prefer it. It's a chance to control our schedule, to refuel without interruption. Eating alone preserves our autonomy. In our endless pursuit of personal happiness, it seems like a good choice, maximizing tranquility while minimizing the hassles that people bring with them. Do we miss their company? Not really.

We're doing just fine with our handheld device, the dinner companion of our age.

Internet Individualism

We're living in the age of individualism in the West,[5] and its symbol is our mobile device. This is the air we breathe, and that makes it feel right. After all, who questions the air?

---

3. Barbara Balfour, "Tables for One—The Rise of Solo Dining," *BBC News*, July 24, 2014, http://www.bbc.com/news/business-28292651.

4. "Study Shows Eating Alone Is Bad for Your Health," *Huff/Post 50*, last updated October 30, 2013, http://www.huffingtonpost.com/2013/10/29/loneliness-affects-diet_n_4173944.html.

5. "Ross Douthat, "The Age of Individualism," *New York Times*, March 15, 2014, http://www.nytimes.com/2014/03/16/opinion/sunday/douthat-the-age-of-individualism.html?_r=0.

With my connection to the Internet in hand, I become self-sufficient. I have access to entertainment, to options, and to all the information I could possibly need to solve any question that I could possibly have. I become my own expert.

So, for example, I go to the doctor's office having researched my symptoms by doing several web searches. It's good to be prepared for an office visit, but I've gone way beyond that. Instead of walking in and reporting the symptoms, I pronounce my own diagnosis and ask the doctor if she would please write the prescription I require.

I discount the doctor's eight years of training and subsequent years of experience because I think I know better. What can she know that I, with the world at my fingertips, do not? I see the certificates on her wall, but I don't see the shoulders on which she stands, the generations of researchers and teachers and clinicians and practitioners on which her practice has been built.

Too much eating alone gives me a false sense of expertise. The same thing can happen when I come to my Bible. I may assume that my view is the right one, unless I'm regularly showing up at the shared meal.

GATHERED

God doesn't leave us isolated to figure everything out for ourselves. He gathers us. The shared meal is his idea. He knows that we need to feed on Christ as a family, as well as individually. We don't just need the personal Word; we need the preached Word.

We need to read and hear the Bible with the church, where "Christ is the host and the chef. . . . His ministers are simply waiters delivering to his guests some savory morsels of the Lamb's everlasting wedding feast."[6]

6. Michael Horton, *Ordinary: Sustainable Faith in a Radical, Restless World* (Grand

God gathers us at his table. And then he feeds us.

Hearing the Word Together

We come hungry. The Word has nourished us during the week, but it has also become diluted by our endless inner dialogue. We've grown tired of arguing with ourselves. We need a word from outside us.

That's why God appointed preaching to be the primary way his message—Christ crucified and raised for us—would be given out to us. "Preach the word," he said through Paul to Timothy (2 Tim 4:2) and to the generations of faithful pastors after him (2 Tim. 2:2). That's the external Word that we need.

God provides the preached Word for us in his usual manner—by grace. The ascended Christ pours out gifts not just on individual believers but on the church in the form of its leaders.

"*He gave* the apostles, the prophets, the evangelists, the shepherds and teachers"—why? "To equip the saints for the work of ministry, for building up the body of Christ" (Eph. 4:11–12). To what end? "Until we all attain to the unity of the faith and of the knowledge of the Son of God, to mature manhood, to the measure of the stature of the fullness of Christ" (Eph. 4:13).

He gives us leaders to bring us to unity and maturity. They are tasked with equipping us for works of service. What kind of preached Word can do all that?

The Word of the gospel.

What kind of equipping do we need for our work? Practical how-tos? Motivational messages? The week's list of projects to tackle and problems to solve?

No—the best way for us to prepare for *our work* is to hear once again about *Christ's finished work*. We need to hear that the most important work has already been done, that the massive

Rapids: Zondervan, 2014), 149.

foundation for life has already been laid. Our works of service in the coming week—raising children, researching cancer, helping our neighbor, feeding the homeless—will be placed brick by brick on top of his.

Hearing about Jesus' work right-sizes our work for us. We've been reading about his work all week, but the voice in our heads isn't loud enough. And it sounds suspiciously like our own. We need to hear the good news from someone else.

That's why true faith in Jesus—not just first-time faith, but ongoing faith—"comes from hearing, and hearing through the word of Christ" (Rom 10:17), specifically the preached Word of the gospel.[7]

It's an ordinary tool, made extraordinary by the power of the Holy Spirit.[8]

Two Benefits

All the benefits of Christ come to me by means of the shared meal. But I'd like to highlight two of them: the provision for our disconnectedness and the antidote to our autonomy.

First, I'm no longer alone. Through the shared meal, God addresses my loneliness by placing me in a family. Connected by the indwelling Spirit, we receive Christ, the Word of God, together. Together we hear him preached—not the same condensed version over and over again, but another chapter in the big story. Together we "take and eat"—adding touch and taste as we partake in the Lord's Supper. Together we take Jesus in.

Together we also work out the implications of what we've heard and eaten. The fact is that we need others who have heard,

---

7. "And how are they to hear without someone preaching?" (Rom 10:14).
8. Westminster Shorter Catechism,
   Q: 89: How is the Word made effectual to salvation?
   A: The Spirit of God taketh the reading, but especially the preaching, of the Word, an effectual means of convincing and converting sinners, and of building them up in holiness and comfort, through faith, unto salvation.

been encouraged, experienced conviction, and received mercy to help us to believe and apply the gospel to whatever we're dealing with. We're no longer alone with that, either.

Second, I'm no longer my own expert. Through the shared meal, God addresses my autonomy. At home alone with my Bible and my own thoughts, I can become captive to my personal biases. I can miss the gospel if I tend toward legalism. I can hear condemnation in the very verse that was meant to bring me comfort. Or I can use the Bible to justify the craving I've already decided to pursue. I can come up with private interpretations that slide toward one of the old heresies. Personal study is good, but my interpretations need to be confirmed by the larger community of faith.

The weekly gospel preaching of a faithful pastor provides an antidote to these temptations of individualism. The pastor stands on the shoulders of translators, interpreters, martyrs, and theologians. He is bound by the creeds. He knows the confessions. He brings me more than his own private interpretations.

Our private world has been brought out into the open. We are now "interpreting Scripture with the larger church rather than thinking of ourselves as omnicompetent."[9]

And we're getting better at understanding our Bibles at home. That's why a recent book on preaching urges pastors to dish out Christ from every text every week. "A steady diet of expository sermons also teaches your audience how to read their own Bibles, how to think through a passage and figure it out. . . . They become savvier and more sensitive readers in their own study."[10]

We need that kind of preaching, and we need to hear it together.

9. Michael Horton, *A Better Way: Rediscovering the Drama of Christ-Centered Worship* (Grand Rapids: Baker, 2002), 90.

10. Timothy Keller, *Preaching: Communicating Faith in an Age of Skepticism* (New York: Viking, 2015), 38.

SHARING WITH EACH OTHER

When we make something tasty, we love to share it. We bring it to the break room at the office or leave a plateful in the teachers' lounge or take some to our play date at the park or hand out little bags to our walking group. It cheers us as well as others when we do.

Spiritual food can be shared too, bringing joy to both the giver and the recipient, but it doesn't always feel as easy.

Have you ever been disappointed with the quality of conversation you have with other believers? It can seem so easy to talk about anything from sales to succulents—anything but Jesus.

Sometimes we try to turn the conversation in a spiritual direction with an innocent question like, "So . . . what's God teaching you these days?" But instead of opening the door to a deeper talk, it brings your visit to a sudden halt. "Ummm . . . not much . . . not sure. . . . Well, I've gotta run!"

There are two ways that feeding on Jesus regularly can help us to share the meal with each other—by helping us to taste his goodness and see our brothers' and sisters' hunger.

You Gotta Taste This!

Remember my mall story in the last chapter? When we're chowing down on something delicious, we often spontaneously offer a bite to the people we're with. They don't usually turn us down either.

Why is that? The context is important. We're diners at the same table. We know each other. We trust each other. If someone at the next table offered us a bite, we wouldn't be so quick to hand her our fork.

Also, we can see the obvious pleasure that the food brings our dinner companions. They aren't trying to talk us into anything they aren't already experiencing. We see their offer as a generous one. They've found something really good, and they're not just keeping it for themselves. And we see that they're not asking anything from us. They aren't vendors hoping to sell us something by offering a free sample.

The first way we share, then, is by simply savoring Jesus ourselves. When we taste his goodness firsthand through a sermon or our personal study, we roll it around on our tongues and let it dissolve. We think about it again and again. We revel in it. That makes us primed to talk about it.

I was in a small group Bible study that was talking about Psalm 1 and the value of meditating on Scripture. "How are we like a tree?" the leader asked, referring to the metaphor in verse 3: "He is like a tree planted by streams of water that yields its fruit in its season, and its leaf does not wither." We shared our answers.

Then a woman spoke up. She had obviously been thinking about this for some time.

"I became a Christian because of a tree. I'd never noticed nature much, but when God began to work in me, the first thing I noticed was trees, especially a certain tree near my house. I would stop and stare at it—its size, its beauty, its strength, its rootedness. A tree doesn't have to do anything, it just is. It provides shelter and food for so many creatures by just being what it was made to be. After I believed, I read this psalm, and God used it to reassure me. 'That's you. I've made you a tree.'"

What she shared came from deep within her and went deep into each of us. It was the Word of Christ dwelling in her richly and then feeding us too.[11]

You Look Hungry

A week or so later, I was talking with a woman from our church who was quite distressed. A mom at her kids' school

---

11. "Let the word of Christ dwell in you richly, teaching and admonishing one another in all wisdom, singing psalms and hymns and spiritual songs, with thankfulness in your hearts to God" (Col 3:16).

had become a widow when her husband had committed suicide. My friend was undone. She knew the woman well and wanted to help her, but she was overwhelmed by the enormity of the situation.

I promised to pray as she asked, but I could tell that she felt her utter lack of ability to say or do anything that would really help. I searched for words to give her. Then I remembered.

"Don't worry about saying or doing the right thing. God has made you like a tree . . ." I went on to share with her the truth of Psalm 1 and the picture of her being used by God to shelter and nourish this friend over time, simply by being there as a believer who was rooted in Jesus Christ.

I was able to share the Word with her because I had tasted it first and then because I had noticed that she was hungry.

When the Word of Christ dwells in us richly, we can hand it out to other believers who we see are hungry. We can be the external word that they need to hear when the word inside them grows faint or is drowned out by other voices.

Pastor and martyr Dietrich Bonhoeffer wrote about our need to hear Christ from each other:

> Therefore the Christian needs another Christian who speaks God's Word to him. He needs him again and again when he becomes uncertain and discouraged, for by himself he cannot help himself without belying the truth. He needs his brother man as a bearer and proclaimer of the divine word of salvation. He needs his brother solely because of Jesus Christ. The Christ in his own heart is weaker than the Christ in the word of his brother; his own heart is uncertain his brother's is sure.[12]

12. Dietrich Bonhoeffer, *Life Together*, trans. John W. Doberstein (New York: Harper & Row, 1954), 23.

My friend already knew Psalm 1. She had read about the tree. But she needed to hear it from someone outside herself.

FEEDING THE HUNGRY

But what about sharing this food with our friends who are outside the Christian faith?

When I've seen a really good movie, I can't help talking about it. It's on my mind, so it comes out of my mouth. "Have you seen _____ yet?" If the answer is yes, we start trading favorite parts and end up enjoying the movie more because we have shared it. If the answer is no, I fill in the basic plot (minus spoilers), cite some of my favorite moments, and end with a promotion. "You've gotta see it on the big screen. It's worth the full price."

I want all my friends to see the movie and enjoy it as much as I did. The insiders have already seen it and know that it's good. The outsiders haven't seen it yet, but I want them to.

What I'm thinking about is usually what I want to talk about. That's why immersing myself in the gospel story makes me want to talk about Jesus, not just with insiders to the faith but with outsiders too.

Only One Gospel

Without realizing it, insiders can live as if we believe in two gospels: one for the outsider and a different one for the insider. We picture Christianity like a private club whose public face is a closed door. To get in, you need to know the password: "Believe in the Lord Jesus Christ and you will be saved." But once inside, you start paying dues, learning the rules, getting busy with projects, and trying to stay out of trouble.

That's the two-gospel myth. It's not the true story.

The true story is that Jesus is the only Savior for all of us. The churchgoer and the "Sunday is fun day" enthusiast. The "most likely to believe" and the unlikely convert. The one who is close to God and the one who stays as far away as possible. The insider and the outsider.

God sent his Son to save sinners. Period. We all need him to save us and to keep saving us until we are safely home, so he designed a plan for salvation that doesn't end until we get there.

How he's rescuing me today from my sins and sorrows is the scene of the gospel drama that's currently playing in my mind. Like the day I forgot to pick up not just my own daughter but also my neighbor's.

It was a junior high moment for all of us. On Friday night, the two girls decided that they needed to celebrate the weekend by adorning a fellow classmate's trees with toilet paper. We mothers had a powwow and decided it was harmless fun, so she promised to drop them off on her way to dinner. I was charged with picking them up.

I would have, except I fell sound asleep on the couch. I woke up with a start several hours later and made a mad dash to the street corner where we were supposed to meet. The girls weren't there. Several minutes that felt like hours later, I discovered that they had walked in the dark to a friend's house and reached the other mom at the restaurant. She had left the table to bring them home.

Whew! They were safe. Oh no. My neighbor, who didn't know Jesus, was shaking with justifiable rage. What could I do?

Apologize, of course, but as I prayed for the right words to say, the gospel became active in the situation. I was a worse mom than I had realized. I was the kind of mom who left her child (and a neighbor's) on a dark street corner for hours. But God already knew that, and Jesus was saving me from that right now. He had kept the girls from harm, *and* he had paid for my negligence on the cross and given me his perfect record of taking care of his children. My apology to the mom came from a deeply humbled, newly forgiven heart.

Jesus turns my worst moments into the best news. That's what I have to share with others.

Honest Need, Only Savior

I can be honest about my weaknesses, even about my failures, because of the finished work of Christ. My honesty doesn't come naturally; it is supernatural. I face the worst about myself at the cross of Christ. But at the same moment, I look up and see love in the face of the one who died for me. That makes me humble and confident at the same time.

My honesty with weakness often opens the door for honest conversation with my neighbor. We understand each other. We're in this leaky boat together. But I have more to offer her than the camaraderie of mutual honesty—an "I'm okay; you're okay" moment. Instead, my need shows off the Savior who can rescue us both.

The food I share is food that I've tasted first.

PLENTY

We're coming to the end of our journey from hunger to plenty.

Our hunger is meant to be satisfied not by our own efforts but by the generosity of a God who freely gives us everything we need, even when we don't yet know that we need it. That's why he gave us his Son long before any of us knew or would admit that we needed him.

We hunger for life. Life with a capital *L*. Life at the fullest. We all taste moments of being fully alive along the way—falling in love, seeing the Grand Canyon, laughing with friends until our stomachs hurt, smelling the first whiff of spring, tasting the first cookie hot out of the oven. But those moments don't last.

God gave us his Son so that we would have life in its fullness, starting now and lasting forever—a life of knowing him and finally knowing ourselves in him, through Jesus. That's the gospel. The entire Bible speaks that gospel to every area of our lives, including our hunger.

God's grace in Christ Jesus turns our scarcity into his plenty. It comes to us in two installments—plenty now and plenty later.

Plenty Now—Participation

We've learned that we're not the heroes of the story. We've learned to set our story aside so that we can listen to God's story, in which Jesus is the Hero of Heroes. But God doesn't leave us as spectators; he brings us in.

Through faith in Christ, we become participants in his story.

When Jesus multiplied five loaves and two fish into a feast for five thousand families, he didn't tell his disciples to stand back and watch while he waved a magic wand. He said, "You feed them," and then he multiplied the bread so that they could hand it out.

The family thirteen rows back took food from the hand of Peter or Andrew or Philip. As far as they were concerned, that disciple fed them. And, in a sense, he did, by putting feet to Jesus' words. The disciples walked through the crowds, handing out food. They gathered up the leftovers, a basket each.

They got sweaty and tired, but they got to participate in a scene that was far beyond any they could ever have imagined.

As we sit and feed on the word of the gospel in the Scriptures, we're fueled for our own participation in the story. Whether we get up to change a diaper (for a screaming child who can't treat his painful rash without our help) or to change medicine (for a patient with torn cartilage that won't heal without our scientific discovery),[13] we are bringing the words on the page to life. We are actors performing the script.

13. Both incidents describe acts of service by women in our church.

The book of Acts describes the beginning of this participation. Guided by Word and Spirit, we who come later are written into God's story again and again.

Grasping this vision clarifies and elevates our daily work. When the settlers left England for Jamestown in 1622, pastor and poet John Donne gave them this charge: "The Acts of the Apostles were to convey that name of Christ Jesus, and to propagate his Gospel all over the world. Beloved, you are Actors upon the same stage too. The uttermost parts of the earth are your scene. Act out the acts of the apostles."[14]

I may not be the star of the show, but I am participating in something bigger than me right now.

Plenty Later—Satisfaction

As I participate, my hunger is continually transformed so that it can be completely satisfied in the end.

When I was eight, I already had crushes on a dozen boys and couldn't imagine having to pick one for a husband. When I was twelve, I desperately wanted to be a cheerleader. When I was sixteen, I longed to be the next Liza Minnelli and belt out songs with all my heart.

Our hungers change constantly during the timeline of our lives.

Then our personal timeline comes into contact with God's. At the cross of Christ, they intersect. Will you and I kneel and weep or turn and walk away? Faith in Christ—which itself is a gift—makes the intersection a permanent meeting place. God brings my timeline, hungers and all, into his. My hungers are known. Evaluated. Purified. Made true.

True hunger is always blessed because it will be finally satisfied—not just barely, not just partially, but fully and finally.

---

14. Quoted in Kevin J. VanHoozer, *Faith Speaking Understanding: Performing the Drama of Doctrine* (Louisville, KY: Westminster John Knox Press, 2014), frontispiece.

God comes to us in his Word to accomplish this task before the final day when he returns in person.

On that day, Jesus will come to us in heroic strength and breathtaking beauty. We will see the one whom our souls love, and seeing, we will be transformed in an instant into the glorious beauty we had always hoped for—every spot removed, every blemish healed. We will be ushered immediately into the fullness of our union with Christ, the union that began when we first believed. As his beloved bride, we will fall into his arms. Forever.

Then the party will begin.

The man whose first earthly miracle was to change water into wine will throw open the doors to his own wedding feast, the marriage supper of the Lamb. We will enter and celebrate with a joy that can't be expressed in the words available to us now.

Last New Year's Eve, my husband and I attended a wedding in a historic Spanish chapel in Balboa Park, San Diego. We were amazed to have been invited, since we were outsiders to the clan that assembled from all over the country. After the tender ceremony, the guests filed outside where, to our surprise, we were greeted by a bagpiper.

He took the lead, followed by the bride and groom, and we processed to a lively jig through the sparkling Christmas lights of the park to a restaurant where we would begin our celebration. Toasting, feasting, dancing, laughing. Party hats, horns, the countdown to midnight.

It was a wedding feast that culminated in a New Year. I've never been to a party like it.

Blessed are those who are invited to the marriage supper of the Lamb. (Rev. 19:9)

Blessed are those who hunger and thirst for righteousness, for they shall be satisfied. (Matt 5:6)

FOR REFLECTION AND DISCUSSION

1. Why is "me and my Bible" not enough? What has been your own experience of hearing the Word from your pastor and from others?
2. Read Romans 10:13–17. Trace the path that Paul lays out from verse 13 to verse 17 with his series of questions.
3. How does tasting the gospel ourselves help us to share it with others—both outsiders and insiders?
4. "Through faith in Christ, we become participants in his story" (p. 241). What does your own participation look like?
5. Pause and imagine your own hungers being finally purified and completely satisfied. Worship and give thanks.

Acknowledgments

I'm thankful for the opportunity to write this book. If it had been a pregnancy, the gestation period would have exceeded that of any known land animal. I'm so glad to get it out of my head and into your hands.

Elyse Fitzpatrick opened the door for me into the publishing world. P&R was willing to take a chance on me. Amanda Martin, my editor, skillfully guided me from my early queasiness to the final delivery. Her steady encouragement and incisive questions brought out the best in me. Thank you.

A string of pastors and theologians have helped me to see Jesus better in the Scriptures and to not be content with anything less than a faith-sight of him—from Tim Keller to my current pastors, David Nutting, Bradley Arekelian, and Joel Fitzpatrick, to my favorite pastor (and husband), Mark Lauterbach, whom I follow all over the county. Thank you.

A group of friends and family have put up with weekly e-mails for prayer support. Many of them also read and gave valuable feedback to each chapter so that I wasn't just talking to myself as I wrote—Emily Ruch (my mom), Emily Ruch (my sister), Bobby and Lisa Ruch (my brother and his wife), Lensa Woodcock, Meredith Bowman, Laura Stenhouse, Ko Matsuo, Julie Witskin, Crystal Moran-Gutierrez, Erin Culp, Tiana Palmer,

Erin Horpayak, Linda DeBerry, Kirsten Woerner, Becky Priest, Cheryl Larson, and Wendy MacLean. Thank you.

My children, Rachel, David, and Rebecca; their spouses, Jeremy, Sonya, and Alex; and my grandchildren, Brendon, Emily, Abi, and Emil, supplied illustrations and stories and put up with my occasional embellishments. They've come to expect it. Thank you.

My husband thought the third child would be my last pregnancy. Little did he know that he would be supporting me through the mood swings and meltdowns of this one. Our long Monday walks solved many theological and editorial dilemmas, a direct result of his expertise and generous love. Thank you.

Appendix A

Philemon Worksheets

WORKSHEET 1: PREPPING THE PASSAGE

1. *What happens here?* Read the entire letter and write a one-to-two-sentence summary that gives the simple facts of the story. (You might use the questions *who, what, when, where,* and *how,* but avoid the question *why.*)

_____

_____

_____

_____

_____

_____

_____

2. *What does it tell me about God?* Focus on the body of the letter, verses 8–20. Observe every mention of God and note what you learn about him: his character, his words, his actions. (If these stir any personal questions you want to ask God, write those in the margin.)

_____

_____

_____

_____

_____

_____

_____

_____

_____

_____

_____

3. *What does it tell me about the people?* Focus on the body of the letter—verses 8–20. Observe Paul first. What do you learn about him? Can you picture him? Then do the same with Philemon and Onesimus. Is anyone a hero, villain, sinner, or sufferer? (If you identify with one person more than the others, make a note in the margin.)

_____

_____

_____

_____

_____

_____

_____

_____

_____

_____

4. *What's the relationship between God and Paul? Between God and Philemon? Between God and Onesimus?* (If anything surprises you about how God relates to each one, put a question mark in the margin.)

_____

_____

_____

_____

_____

_____

_____

_____

_____

_____

_____

WORKSHEET 2: SEEING JESUS, THE MISSING INGREDIENT

1. Which of the eight shortcuts is present in this passage? Pick one and write it here.

God's	Man or Woman as
1. Character	5. Hero
2. Commands	6. Villain
3. Promises	7. Sinner
4. Mercy	8. Sufferer

2. Ask the follow-up question to the shortcut you chose. See the charts below. Write it here.

Do I see . . .	How does Jesus . . .	Verse
1. a character quality of God here?	make this aspect of God's character visible?	"He is the image of the invisible God" (Col. 1:15).
2. a command of God here?	make this command beautiful, not crushing?	"I have not come to abolish [the Law and the Prophets] but to fulfill them" (Matt. 5:17).
3. a promise of God here?	guarantee this promise?	"For all the promises of God find their Yes in him" (2 Cor. 1:20).
4. a mercy of God here?	satisfy God's justice so that God can show mercy here?	"But God, being rich in mercy . . . made us alive together with Christ" (Eph. 2:4–5).

Do I see . . .	How does Jesus . . .	Verse
5. man or woman as hero here?	exceed this person's words, actions, or virtues?	"Behold, something greater than Solomon is here" (Luke 11:31).
6. man or woman as villain here?	show that his way is much better?	"For I have no pleasure in the death of anyone, declares the Lord GOD; so turn and live" (Ezek. 18:32).
7. man or woman as sinner here?	bear this sin and its consequences away?	"For our sake he made him to be sin who knew no sin, so that in him we might become the righteousness of God" (2 Cor. 5:21).
8. man or woman as sufferer here?	experience, endure, and redeem this suffering?	"Although he was a son, he learned obedience through what he suffered" (Heb. 5:8).

3. Answer the follow-up question from your own knowledge of Jesus' sinless life and finished work as presented in the New Testament. Write it here. Be specific. (For example, don't settle for a general statement like, "This man was bad and Jesus was good," but ask and answer like this: "How was this man specifically bad, and how did Jesus' goodness specifically match and exceed his badness?")

_____

_____

_____

_____

_____

WORKSHEET 3: FEEDING ON CHRIST

Taste the passage through the questions below.

Eat: Feeding on the Gospel	Question	Verse
Gospel Praise	How is Jesus beautiful and how is his work wonderful to me today?	"Oh, taste and see that the LORD is good!" (Ps. 34:8).
Gospel Perspective	How does his gospel change the way I look at my life today?	"But be transformed by the renewing of your mind" (Rom. 12:2).
Gospel Provision	How will God provide for me today through Jesus?	"And my God will supply every need of yours according to his riches in glory in Christ Jesus" (Phil. 4:19).

1. How is Jesus beautiful and how is his work wonderful to me today? _____

   _____

   _____

2. How does the gospel change the way I look at my life today?

   _____

   _____

   _____

3. How will God provide for me today through Jesus?

   _____

   _____

4. What is my takeaway verse from today's reading?

   _____

Appendix B

Feeding on Christ
Daily Worksheet

Today's Scripture: _____

PREP: CUTTING UP THE PASSAGE

1. What happens here (and what happened just before this text)?

   _____
   _____
   _____

2. What does this text tell me about God, his character, his words, and his actions?

   _____
   _____
   _____

3. What does the text tell me about people? Do I see a hero, villain, sinner, or sufferer here?

   _____
   _____
   _____

4. What is the relationship between God and the people?

   _____
   _____

COOK: ADDING THE MISSING INGREDIENT

5. Look for one of these ingredients in the passage. How does it point me to Jesus?

   • God's Character

   • God's Commands

- God's Promises

- God's Mercy

- A Hero

- A Villain

- A Sinner

- A Sufferer

EAT: TASTING THE THREE-COURSE MEAL

6. Gospel Praise. How are Jesus beautiful and his work wonderful to me today?

_____

_____

_____

7. Gospel Perspective. How does Jesus' gospel change the way I look at my life today?

_____

_____

_____

8. Gospel Provision. How will God provide for me today through Jesus?

_____

_____

_____

Takeaway Verse: _____

Rondi Lauterbach earned an AB from Princeton University, where she studied Russian, and an MA from Portland State University, where she learned to teach English. She has been married to Mark, a pastor, since 1978 and is a mother of three and grandmother of four, as well as a Bible study leader, Pilates teacher, and fierce competitor at all board games.

As a pastor's wife, Rondi has been a friend and encourager to women in their life's callings. Her journey to find true satisfaction for her own hunger began during her struggles to navigate life through marriage, babies, cross-country moves, and ministry. Her husband encouraged her to think long term and to invest her time regularly in Bible study, and those early years convinced her of two things: that God knows the true hunger of our hearts, and that he delights to feed us with his Word.

Decades later, Rondi encountered the Christ-centered hermeneutic of the Bible through the preaching and teaching of Ed Clowney and others. Now she is eager to share this good news and equip others with the tools to see Jesus for themselves and be transformed by his saving work.